The Chemistry of LEADERSHIP

A Self-Discovery Formula to
Finding the Leader in You

Finding the "elements" within yourself and blending
them to create an inspiring "reaction",
resulting in meaningful and impactful outcomes.

Paul E. Fein

My Story of Discovery

outskirts
press

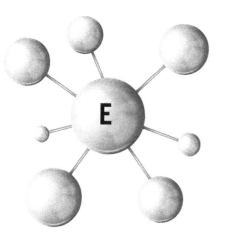

ENDORSEMENTS

Praise for *The Chemistry of LEADERSHIP*

A Self-Discovery Formula to Finding the Leader in You

Finding the "elements" within yourself and blending them to create an inspiring "reaction", resulting in meaningful and impactful outcomes.

Many authors have tried to summarize great leadership. This book is one of the absolutely best approaches that I have ever seen to build powerful leadership through self-awareness. Paul elegantly divides "The Chemistry of Leadership" into eight competencies including 13 support components. I am specifically impressed with the chemistry approach of looking inward to be able to act outward. It wouldn't surprise me if this book becomes the leadership book of the year in 2018.

Anders Hedin, PhD., Ass. Professor
International Leadership Consultant
Dinovation SE
Stockholm, Sweden

Having worked with Paul for several years, I have never seen any leader that is so engaging and authentic as Paul. It is fantastic to see him now sharing his experiences in a leadership book so that others can read about his learning journey. He has an excellent level of self-awareness along with a true focus on people. Clearly, leadership is based on cross-cultural agility and human engagement.

Magnus Lundback
Executive Vice President, HR & Sustainability
Getinge
Gothenburg, Sweden

Paul's book, "The Chemistry of Leadership", is an honest and heartfelt account by a true visionary who is passionate about people and the tremendous potential that we all possess to grow and achieve amazing success both as individuals and as members of our society.

This book is a well-balanced mix of all the elements needed by leaders of today and tomorrow to deliver outstanding results while providing holistic guidance to others, and in the end, enhancing the standard of living of our communities.

Roberto Concha
President
Executive Search & Leadership Talent Acquisition
Mexico / Brazil / Latin America
Los Angeles, California

Wow! A heartfelt and inspiring read on the key elements that make a great leader.

Paul's passion and in-depth knowledge from multiple backgrounds really shines through in this engaging book. A must for any leader looking to go on a journey of self-discovery, enhancing their capabilities and adding some "human chemistry" into their leadership relationships.

> *Rachael Forsberg*
> *Executive Coach & Leadership Consultant*
> *London, England*

I have had the privilege of working with Paul for the past 17 years. There has never been a moment where he has not conveyed his passion for working with and developing leaders at all levels. Paul has an innate ability to allow individuals the opportunity to self-reflect and identify the leader within themselves. His coaching style is one of best that I have personally experienced. All leaders regardless of their capabilities, will be able to gain something from his life lessons. As Paul has so eloquently stated throughout my discussions with him; "Leadership is a continuous learning journey of which you never stop learning".

This is a must read for anyone in leadership.

> *Therese Mueller*
> *President*
> *Getinge – Canada*
> *Mississauga, Ontario*

Business books should be easy to read, easy to understand and most importantly, easy to apply. Paul's book meets all of these criteria in the fullest. The reader can benefit from his years of hands-on experience, both domestically and internationally, and his great writing style. The reader will be in for a wonderful journey towards self-discovery. Enjoy the ride!

Thomas Marschall Vice President – Human Resources
Business Area Acute Care Therapies
Getinge – Maquet Holding B.V. & Co.KG
Rastatt, Germany

"The Chemistry of Leadership" creates alchemy for anyone who has the job of leading people – turning Paul's experience and research into developmental gold. His passion for unlocking the leadership potential in all of us shines through on every page. And, his approach of focusing on people before process speaks to his extensive background in organizational development and executive coaching. "The Chemistry of Leadership" guarantees to catalyze positive change in any organization.

Kevin Limbach
Vice President US Operations & Service
TAYLORMADE Golf Company
Carlsbad, California

Paul brings great insights and personal reflections in "The Chemistry of Leadership" to help us see the leadership qualities in ourselves that maybe we did not even know we had. His approach and discovery are key elements in his desire for us to become true leaders in everything we do!

Chris Odom
President – Surgical Workflows
United States of America
Getinge
Rochester, New York

I've known and worked with Paul for over 15 years. He *has been the brightest and most impactful of my career mentors and leadership coaches, particularly when it comes to emotional intelligence, connecting with people and leading by example. His ability to find common ground with diverse groups of leaders and relate with each individual on a human level is remarkable. Paul has the ability to easily connect and collaborate with people from all backgrounds by identifying and appreciating the individual's talents and acknowledging their contribution to their families, job and society regardless, of their rank or task being performed by the individual. I strongly endorse and recommend reading The Chemistry of Leadership to both young and upcoming leaders as well as those who have been successfully leading their entire lives, as Paul's insight will be inspiring and valuable to all.*

John Saavedra
Director of International Sales
ACUMED
Hillsboro, Oregon USA

I know Paul as a lifelong scholar of how to improve leadership capability. With this book, he contributes to the journey himself by giving practical examples about how to enhance leadership skills. The book is a must read for those who wants to learn more about great leadership and strives towards creating organizations with leaders that are driven by high levels of ambition.

Björn Frössevi
Director
Center for Higher Ambition Leadership
Göteborg, Sweden

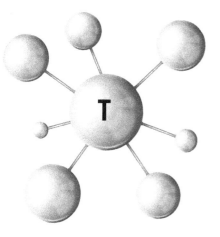

THANKS

An Expression of Appreciation

- To my wife of many years
  ...... for tolerating my unconventional qualities and behaviors.

- To my daughter, Renee, and my son, Eric
  ...... for appreciating my enthusiasm for learning and growing.

- To my many business and personal relationships
  ...... for joining my passionate leadership learning journey.

Leadership is more than an art, a science, or a craft...
It is a life-long learning journey.
It is about *human chemistry.*

TABLE OF CONTENTS

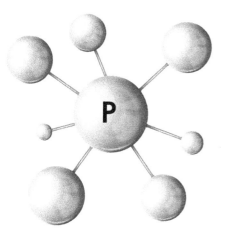

PREFACE

The Chemistry of LEADERSHIP by Paul E. Fein

A Self-Discovery Formula to Finding the Leader in You

Finding the "elements" within yourself and blending them to create an inspiring "reaction", resulting in meaningful and impactful outcomes.

Why read this leadership book?

- The book is informative and inspirational, as well as full of insights and fun.
- It examines eight critical leadership competencies, and explores thirteen key leadership skills.
- It provides the actual application of the leadership competencies, and utilizes supportive models and methodologies.
- It connects theoretic chemistry concepts to human leadership capabilities.
- It employs experiences from teaching and coaching, to global organizational projects.
- It looks at leadership as a life-long learning journey.

Point of interest...

*The **Chemistry** of Leadership*

The definition of chemistry is a science that deals with the form and properties of matter and substances. It is a branch of physical science that studies the composition, structure and changes of matter. It deals with chemical reactions and the principles which govern chemical transformations.

❖ A focus on structure and reactions.
❖ A focus on change and transformation.

*The Chemistry of **Leadership***

The definition of leadership is the encompassing abilities of an individual or an organization to lead other individuals, teams, or an entire organization. Leaders take initiatives, solve problems, find solutions, and build trustworthiness with others through courage and discipline. They have a passion for developing people and energizing others to accomplish innovative as well as inspiring goals.

❖ A focus on accountability, ownership, and dynamic results.
❖ A focus on self-awareness, people compassion, and honesty.

There are many authors that have written outstanding books on leadership and related areas from many diverse perspectives. They are referenced throughout the book.

➢ James C. Collins – *Good to Great – Why Some Companies Make the Leap...and others Don't*
➢ Stephen M.R. Covey – *The Speed of Trust*

- ➢ David Horsager – *The Trusted Edge – How Leaders Gain Faster Results, Deeper Relationships, and a Stronger Bottom Line*
- ➢ Bill George – *True North*
- ➢ Marshall Goldsmith – *What Got You Here Won't Get You There*
- ➢ Patrick Lencioni – *The Five Dysfunctions of a Team*
- ➢ Peter Schwartz – *The Art of the Long View*
- ➢ Judith Umlas – *Grateful Leadership*
- ➢ Sherry Turkle – *Reclaiming Conversations*
- ➢ Joseph Jaworski – *Synchronicity: The Inner Path of Leadership*
- ➢ Max de Pree – *Leadership is an Art*
- ➢ Marshall Goldsmith / Laurence Lyons / Alyssa Frees – *Coaching for Leadership – How the World's Greatest Coaches Help Leaders Learn*
- ➢ Jorge Cuervo – *Leaders Don't Command*
- ➢ Eric Mosley / Derek Irvine – *The Power of Thanks*
- ➢ Amy Cuddy – *Presence – Bringing your Boldest Self to your Biggest Challenges*
- ➢ Frederic Hudson / Pamela McLean – *Life Launch – A Passionate Guide to the Best of your Life*

General Connection and Feedback

I hope this book becomes part of your leadership learning journey and that it helps with finding of the leader in you. Self-reflections drive self-discoveries.

Please do not hesitate to share your thoughts and insights. Feedback comments are of tremendous help in building the next book. Paul

paulefein@gmail.com

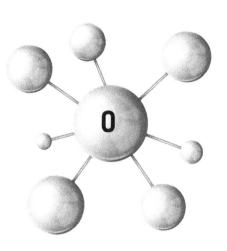

OPENING STORIES

The leadership learning journey based on *human chemistry*.

Spring 2005 – A Leadership Development Workshop in Rome

I had the great privilege of facilitating an interactive leadership learning workshop in a very old hotel in downtown Rome. There were 16 company executives from different parts of the world – Japan, Germany, France, UK, Singapore, and of course, the US. The program started at 8:30 AM on a Tuesday morning in a very spacious conference room that was fantastically decorated and setup for the learning group.

Here is a picture on the flow of events.

"Good morning – I am Paul Fein. Many of you know me quite well, and others are meeting me for the first time. I will be your development program leader for the day."

"Before starting our learning activities, I want you to look up at the ceiling that is about 6 – 8 meters up. Look how beautifully and creatively painted the entire area above our heads has been done with colorfully unique artwork."

As per the participants – "Wow! It is truly amazing – outstanding design and color, surviving many years. Probably painted over 200 years ago."

My next statement was – "Well, that is all we are going to do today."

The responses were – "Are you crazy – I travelled from ...... for this."

Clearly, the executives were shocked, confused, and frustrated.

I responded quickly – "Just kidding" "Look – you are all leaders."

I quickly followed with my insightful remarks and advice so that I could maintain my personal safety.

> "You need to stop every so often and take time to observe your surroundings"

> "You need to connect with your environment, especially with your people."

> "You need to always be real, authentic, open, honest...."

> "And, even as leaders, it is okay to have fun / to have a sense of humor."

> "Basically – lighten up and be human."

> "Leaders need human chemistry – compassion, courage, a connection with others."

> "So, this was your first leader-lesson for today, and going forward, we will be working together on many interactive learning activities."

We proceeded forward and had a full day of learning – many engaging exercises and challenging experiences as part of this leadership learning journey. The executive learners found tremendous value in the connections and self-discoveries they made throughout the day.

Fall 2010 – A Human Resource Group
Development Meeting – Sweden

I facilitated a relationship building group meeting with about thirty Human Resource leaders. They were from several different countries, all a part of the Getinge Group, headquartered in Sweden. This collaborative event occurred over two long days.

To start this dynamic and strategic learning event, I conducted a fun and unique exercise.

"You are all going to receive careful instructions so that you can draw a picture of a running rhinoceros. I will provide you with explicit support and direction."

Everyone was provided with 22 x 28 cm piece of white paper as well as a drawing pencil.

"Proceed with your drawing as follows –

> ➤ First, draw a body and head of the rhino (per a pictorial graphic)
> ➤ Second, add the shoulders onto the body (again, a graphic was briefly shown)
> ➤ Third, add legs
> ➤ Forth, add feet
> ➤ Finally, add a face onto your rhinoceros

"Now – put your name onto your outstanding piece of art."

"Hang your accomplishment on the side wall next to your colleagues' drawings."

Wow! Even though there were many "similar" looking pictures, they were all surprisingly different in many ways."

- Some rhinos were large, others small
- Some rhinos were running to the left, others running to the right
- Some rhinos were very round and robust, others skinny and small
- Some of the drawings were done on the paper in Portrait positions, others, with the paper in Landscape
- Some had their names at the top, others at the bottom
- Some individuals had used only their first name, others, their full name

So, everyone had been provided with the exact same instructions and there was a clear objective to the exercise. The vision was well understood. The participants seemed motivated and inspired to do this fun activity. Yet, the artful creations were different.

Clearly, **human chemistry** can influence results. Leaders need to accept the fact that messages can have different levels of understanding as well as potentially different outcomes. And, leaders must encourage creativity, innovation and ownership, along with active listening and even teamwork. Leadership, without a doubt, is a life-long learning journey.

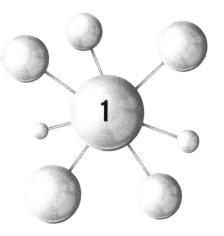

THE INTRODUCTION AND CONNECTION

The Chemistry of LEADERSHIP

A Self-Discovery Formula to Finding the Leader in You

Finding the "elements" within yourself and blending them to create an inspiring "reaction", resulting in meaningful and impactful outcomes.

The Chemistry of LEADERSHIPS is a book focused on a personal leadership learning journey and the leadership competencies used to drive successful business relationships and organizational outcomes.

It looks at the *formula* that enhances individual and organizational effectiveness along with the right *elements and reactions* that are used to build an engaging learning and development culture. Leaders of tomorrow will need to carefully balance the *thinking-&-doing* with the *doing-&-thinking* activities in their leadership roles, and always focus on people as well as performance.

Leadership is more than just a science, more than just an art, and more than just a craft. Leadership is based on **human chemistry** – the ability for a leader to look inward and to become fully self-aware, and the ability for a leader to look outward and to build an understanding of others. Specifically, leaders need to meet the needs of people – employees, managers, directors, colleagues, teams, shareholders, and even external customers and connections. Therefore, the focus of a leader is not on themselves, but on others. Leaders need to communicate openly, listen more, be honest with the facts, have a dynamic vision, and be accountable for their actions. Leaders also need to be compassionate and empathetic, and able to use both emotional and social intelligence to build relationships.

Authentic and agile leadership is based on an energetic focus on people. Raj Sisodia, Jag Sheth, and David Wolfe are authors of **Firms of Endearment – How World-Class Companies Profit from Passion and Purpose.** They state clearly that the heart and spirit of leadership is centered on humans.

> *"A human being is not a resource but a source. A resource is like a lump of coal; once you use it, it's gone, depleted and worn out. A source is like the sun – virtually inexhaustible and continually generating energy, light, and warmth. There is no more powerful source of creative energy in the world than a turned-on, empowered human being." (1)*

There are many questions that leaders need to explore and answered. It is a process of self-reflection and self-discovery, resulting in personal self-awareness.

- What is a leader?
- What is leadership?

- What makes a leader effective?
- What makes a leader successful?
- What makes a leader great?
- What makes a leader authentic?
- What makes a leader trustworthy?
- What makes a leader outstanding?

The General Purpose of the Book

As part of every chapter of *The Chemistry of LEADERSHIP*, the primary discovery and growth experience will be to fully recognize that leadership is a life-long learning journey. The *human chem*istry of leadership is founded on the ability to engage, to communicate, and to connect with people. And, the key for the leader is to always have passion and energy in all leadership activities, regardless of age, work position, or business environment. The learning starts from childhood and continues throughout life as well as one's career. Many competencies are enhanced during the leadership learning journey, and they are constantly reinforced by personal experiences and strong relationships as well as partnerships. Leaders are always building self-awareness and learning to be authentically real – using the mind, touching the heart, and finding the sole.

In each chapter of the book, there will be a connection to many leadership competencies, skills and capabilities. It will be discovered that effective leaders can drive incredible business outcomes and outperform the competition. And, successful company performance is based on building strong and inspiring teams as well as individual organizational members.

A leader with the right *human chemsitry* utilizing many competencies and skills to support their effective leadership behaviors. These human characteristics for effectiveness are driven by high levels of enthusiasm and engagement.

- Leaders need to have clear and dynamic visions that defines goals and direction.

  Team members need to have specific roles and a group mission.

- Leaders need to have an in-depth business acumen and leadership competence.

  Team members need to have fully understand the business and the organizational strategies.

- Leaders need to have a decision-making process based on sound judgment.

  Team members need to have a willingness to impact successful decisions based on detailed evaluation of all information.

- Leaders need to have a level of trust and respect that is established by integrity.

  Team members need to build relationships based on exceptional trustworthiness and personal job satisfaction.

- Leaders need to have a moral compass, show empathy, and demonstrate emotional support for all organizational associates.

  Team members need to accept the weaknesses in their leaders and their vulnerability in a human way.

Both the effective leader and the effective team need to have courage and willingness to take risks outside of the comfort zone. They need to have a strong handle on fear regarding decision-making challenges. And, having courage leads to trust that is based on individual confidence and acceptance of possible failure.

The General Structure and Flow of the Book

This book will help explore several key leadership competencies and provide personal stories specific to self-discoveries throughout my diverse and exciting career. There are nine chapters, each having a similar structure, approach, and flow. There are five components to each chapter.

Component One – The Chemistry Connection – Using actual academic pieces from the world of chemistry and paralleling the scientific facts with specific leadership skills and competencies as well as human behaviors and characteristics.

Component Two – General Remarks on Leadership – Providing opening and engaging thoughts associated with the chapter content that follows. This helps set the stage for self-reflection and encourages self-discovery from the associated learnings.

Component Three – The Leader – Detailing the purpose, passion, and expectations of leadership. This piece is about the aspects of competencies and skills requiring focus by leaders along with their abilities to impact outcomes as well as successful performance. It may even provide insights into established models and deliver details on more than one component of critical leadership competencies.

Component Four – The Personal Story – Sharing and self-disclosing aspects of my personal leadership learning journey. These stories provide insights into my general growth and evolution throughout my career. I hope that these stories demonstrate and encourage the need to engage with people, learn about their needs, develop individual abilities, and find the human chemistry in leadership.

Component Five – General Summary on Leadership – Pulling final thoughts together on the specific competencies and skills, and the potential impact on leading others. These remarks can be inspirational in nature and help drive the utilization of the learnings within the chapter.

Summary Overview of Each Chapter

<u>Chapter One</u> – The Introduction and Connection

This chapter provides insights into the purpose, structure, and flow of the book.

<u>Chapter Two</u> – Leadership and Organizational Values / Corporate Culture

Leaders with core values that define the company culture.

This chapter provides insights into the importance of having well-defined organizational values that drive a focus on both short-term and long-term objectives. The values serve as the foundation for the desired company culture specific to behaviors, attitudes, and leadership practices. Core values will vary from organization to organization. The culture will also evolve over time. Yet, the two key success factors built into the core values and culture are always trust and purpose.

<u>Chapter Three</u> – Leadership and Critical Thinking / Courage

Leaders as drivers of problem-solving, decision-making, and risk-taking.

This chapter provides insights into five areas that are based on intellectual disciple and courage. Using risk-oriented judgment with confidence can help a leader rise above their fears, utilize courage, and handle business challenges successfully.

Chapter Four – Leadership and Authentic Influencing / Emotional Intelligence

Leaders using the power to change the thinking of people and behaviors.

This chapter provides insights into the ability to influence organizational results through authentic and engaging leadership. Leaders are able to create followers that take charge, collaborate, and drive the direction of the company. The emotional intelligence of the leader supports the connection to the soft side of time management, decision-making, and trust building.

Chapter Five – Leadership and Dynamic Relationships

Leaders building connections with employees, teams, and customers.

This chapter provides insights into building relationships and collaborative connections. Positive interactions can result in enhanced strategies and in deeper thinking perspectives. Leaders need to be genuine and authentic in the appreciation of all types of business partnerships.

Chapter Six – Leadership and Communications from the Head and the Heart

Leaders as great connectors, conversationalists, and relationship builders.

This chapter provides insights into the importance of effective communications. Strong interpersonal and social skills can enhance connections and encourage feedback along with active listening. Again, the self-awareness by the leader can drive communication from an emotional level with inspirational confidence and energetic reality.

Chapter Seven – Leadership and Interpersonal Connection

Leaders building coaching cultures and active listening environments.

This chapter provides insights into the importance of engaging employees and into being coach-leaders that can build a focus on company challenges. Gaining a connection to a coaching process and powerful listening abilities can result in effecting tangible as well as intangible business results.

Chapter Eight – Leadership and Business Knowledge / Capabilities

Leaders enhancing employee engagement through different leadership styles.

This chapter provides insights into using business knowledge and leadership strengths to drive and inspire business actions. Leaders are continuously growing and building their own personal leadership style based on their general communication approach and analytical thinking experiences. And, successful performance is enhanced by an enthusiastic and engaged employee workforce that follows a culture of openness, trust, and respect.

Chapter Nine – Leadership and Wisdom

Leaders committed to people and human chemistry.

This chapter provides insights and wisdom into leadership that is founded on human chemistry and the ability of a leader to meet the needs of people by focusing on others, not themselves. Leaders need to balance open humility and assertive energy so that they can ignite innovative curiosity along with long-term commitments. And, leaders need courage to look at all business challenges with a willingness to be vulnerable as well as to take responsibility for risks.

Well...let us start your leadership learning journey. And take some time to do self-reflecting, since it will lead to many personal self-discoveries.

Discover that the learning and growing leaders are fully aware that their roles are to serve people. They need to be authentically open, completely supportive of others and their ideas, and be driven by personal humility. Leaders with high levels of self-awareness are willing to take full ownership of their responsibilities. And, they are willing and able to accept constructive feedback on performance and personal behaviors. Successful and effective leaders are always focused on growing people and on building a strong organization by enhancing the capabilities of employees and colleagues. Leaders are on a leadership learning journey, growing their competencies and stretching themselves to be able to impact business outcomes.

Look to find personal value in this journey.

Inspiration
To inspire a desire to develop personal self-awareness specific to leadership competencies and skills.

Development
To build and enhance effective leadership capabilities and behaviors throughout the learning journey.

Discovery
To stimulate self-discovery by authentically being people-focus with strong connections and communications.

Kindness
To grow and touch the heart by driving confidence, trust, and personal humility as well as active listening based on openness and transparency.

Appreciation
To gain empowerment that establishes mutual accountability for actions and for recognition of accomplishments.

Loyalty
To develop energetic and enthusiastic teamwork with a pride for excellence and the desire to tackle challenges.

Performance
To drive business successes and outcomes based on clear insights into strategic targets, through business savvy, and building cultural transformations.

Partnerships
To find honest presence and compelling sincerity through trust, compassion, and spirit in relationships.

Leadership requirements and expectations will continue to evolve in our complex work environments and global marketplaces. There will be a need for higher levels of flexibility and the use of different leadership styles to be able to address new organizational challenges and new strategic opportunities. Leaders will always be building people relationships and enhancing the flow of personal communication, and even reducing the addiction to electronic devices.

Leadership is about people...the *human chemistry*!

- Leaders need to listen.
- Leaders need to care.
- Leaders need to celebrate successes.

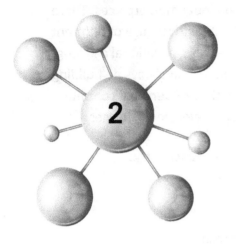

2

LEADERSHIP AND ORGANIZATIONAL VALUES / CORPORATE CULTURE

Leaders with core values that define the company culture.

The Chemistry Connection

The atoms or molecules that make up chemical structures can have different arrangements as well as physical properties, such as color, crystal shapes, hardness, and melting points. Allotropes are different physical forms of the same atoms. Diamonds and graphite are two allotropes of carbon atoms. Both have different bonds, with diamonds having no free electrons since they all are involved in the bonding. Therefore, diamonds are the hardest known substance, and graphite is extremely soft.

Core values define the behaviors and practices of company leaders and the employee population. They serve as the foundation and philosophy of the organizational culture along with the supporting business environment. Even though most core values, such as integrity and trust, are similar from company-to-company, the corporate cultures and desired leadership competencies can be dramatically different. And, organizational strategies, managerial styles, visions and missions, and even budgetary constraints, all can further define the workplace culture. Basically, same "value elements" can be connected back to different levels of corporate engagement and managerial philosophies.

General Remarks on Leadership

Leadership is built on human connections as well as human presence. Leadership is founded on a diversity of competencies and skills such as integrity, compassion, empathy, humility, and openness. It is the leader that establishes an inspiring vision and utilizes their personal behaviors to demonstrate the desired core values and compelling principles for an organization. These core company values become the guiding drivers of an engaged workforce that results in successful business outcomes.

Organizational Core Values and Culture

Organizational values define and impact the behaviors and practices of leaders, the employee population, and the company culture. They are critical in the enforcement of actions and the actual execution of specific goals that are used in building priorities and strategies. They also serve as general communication filters. Core values create and help drive a focus on both the short-term and long-term objectives. They define the paths to deliver impactful results as well as to find business solutions that support key transformations.

So, the core organizational values serve as the foundation for the desired company culture along with the behaviors and attitudes of the employees, and even define the practices of leaders. These values enhance the *human chemistry* and characteristics of leadership for business success.

Leaders continue to develop and grow throughout their learning journey by:

- Building personal self-awareness
- Enhancing empathy, humility, and integrity
- Driving higher levels of openness
- Finding inner generosity, love, and wisdom
- Creating respect
- Finding grit and determination
- Having courage and conviction

Core values become the guiding principles that are used to define the enduring character and composition of an organization. As already stated, they serve as the foundation for the desired behaviors in the form of a *code of conduct*. They create a philosophical identity that can be used to shape the organization as it evolves and grows over time. And, on a daily basis, employees at all levels of the company are using the values and demonstrating their beliefs specific to their responsibilities and to their flow of communications with others.

As per James C. Collins (author of **Good to Great**) and Jerry I. Porras in their article that appeared in the Harvard Business Review:

"Core values are the essential and enduring tenets of an organization.

A small set of timeless guiding principles that require no external justification; they have intrinsic value and importance to those inside the organization." (1)

Core values become the framework for leaders as the company achieves the established goals and strategies of the organization. They evolve into procedures, ethical expectations, and even into the creation of a well-defined work environment and general atmosphere. They become a way of life along with emotional rules that are used in problem-solving and decision-making. New standards for excellence and expectations for all employees continue to evolve. They become the building blocks for loyalty and motivation as the behaviors become embedded into the organizational culture.

Ten potential core values

There are many potential core values that can be used to define the actual practices and attitudes of the leaders of the company and the employee population. The following value areas can potentially be used to establish a core organizational culture. The key is to recognize that the focus on people must be the primary and critical driver of the *human chemistry* utilized by inspiring leaders.

Trust and Integrity

Being open and honest, demonstrating high levels of ethics, embracing congruence in thoughts, feelings, and actions. Credibility, earned confidence and professional consistency builds relationships, drives respect, and enhances loyalty. Trust is the foundation for the most desirable organizational outcomes, such as productivity, job satisfaction, and company commitment.

Quality and Excellence

Establishing high standards, being best-in-class, and searching for new ways to improve. Intellectual consistency based on a long-term perspective helps embrace change, find solutions, and enhance customer satisfaction. This can be accomplished by exceeding expectations and achieving superior performance through all forms of quality.

Risk Taking and Courage

Accepting challenges, willing to go outside of the comfort zone, and learning from mistakes. Choices need to be made and being vulnerable is completely acceptable, especially when imagination and creativity are not sacrificed. Pursuing big goals may require some adjustments and a risk-taking willingness, along with a significant level of determination.

Communication and Inspiration

Listening and communicating effectively, building an understanding of different perspectives, and driving a passion for goals, objectives and a compelling vision. A high level of openness is demonstrated through active listening, accepting feedback, addressing conflicts, and engaging with others from the heart. Sharing ideas with sincerity can enhance presence, drive a sense of purpose, and achieve break through results.

Development and Growth

Fostering a learning environment, allocating time and resources, and aligning personal growth with business outcomes. Having a focus on performance and the ability to contribute demonstrates the corporate commitment to growing skills and competencies needed for the future.

Ownership and Accountability

Delivering on promises, prioritizing responsibilities and demonstrating personal drive and commitment. There is a leadership conviction to build insights and knowledge about the business and the employee population. Careful planning, decision-making, and decisive actions all fully utilize the diversity of teams and the willingness to empower others.

Humility and Pride

Humbleness, honesty, empathy, and compassion. Emotional intelligence supports the spirit, energy and enthusiasm for accepting challenges along with a positively optimistic focus on change. It demonstrates personal self-confidence and the value in others.

Teamwork and Collaboration

Partnering, sharing of knowledge and information, and being action oriented. Supportive approaches can lead to outstanding outcomes, even when obstacles surface. Inclusion drives engagement, and empowerment builds enthusiasm along with commitment.

Appreciation and Acknowledgment

Focusing on the contributions made by people and celebrating achievements. Reaching high levels of excellence is driven by rewarding and recognizing strong performance as well as contributions to the organization.

Transparency and Openness

Building on all aspects of authenticity and truthfulness. Consideration for diversity and demonstrating realism drives true inspiration for awareness and a genuine understanding of the needs of others. It shows courage, flexibility, open-mindedness, and non-judgmental behaviors.

There are many core values that can define the behaviors, attitude and beliefs of the employee population as well as the practices of the company leaders. And, eventually, the selected values become the connection to a common organizational culture. Leaders must inspire the engagement and the commitment to the core values, and in turn, to the company. Effective and influential leaders are always *balancing two major capability characteristics and practices* – their ability to build trust in all relationships, and their ability to drive a positive and energizing organizational purpose.

Authentic Trust and Compassionate Integrity

Leaders need to always remain sincerely focused on enhancing their credibility and trust. By being genuine and real individuals, leaders grow relationships into partnerships. Positive connections clearly drive commitment, loyalty and collaboration. Leaders that are willing to be vulnerable, even be wrong at times, can encourage the unique value of being humble and being fully present.

Leader are always learning and evolving throughout their leadership journey. They are able to promote personal trust by "leading-by-example" and "walking-the-talk". Their authentic and realistic leadership mindset as well as actions are based on self-confidence and active listening. Leaders need to embrace their roles with optimism and enthusiasm. This builds respect and compassion for differences throughout the work environment. And, leaders must always be professional connectors and powerful influencers in their communications and behaviors.

Clear Purpose and a Passionate Vision

By building stronger and passionate cultures with clear processes, leaders are able to surpass goal expectations and to maximize results. Relationships and work teams that are based on positive work environments as well as on a specific purpose can encourage the formation and utilization of a shared and collective vision. Establishing outstanding values along with innovative thinking, helps the organization to become more strategic in nature, and to motivate ways of address challenges in a creative fashion. This can occur both through extrinsic as well as intrinsic behaviors and attitudes. An optimistic and uplifting purpose can enhance productivity, drive sustainable results, and raise profitability along with revenue growth.

An inspiring vision with a clear purpose energizes people. The vision built on current business objectives and critical goals, establishes the direction to where the organization needs to go, and to what the organizations needs to become. This optimal "picture" defines specific desires, potential end results, possible consequences, and even a dream to strive to be successful. How is this vision and mission achieved? By having specific methods and strategies, both domestically and globally. This supports the "why", the purpose behind all breakthrough actions, long-term changes, and a courageous future direction. Removing ambiguity in the values and culture will drive aspiring, realistic, and achievable organizational successes. Employees become more engaged and more motivated to build higher levels of productivity. Leaders that are "living" the purpose, vision and strategic plans, are seen as encouraging and supporting successful achievements and contributions.

The "flow" and "value" of balancing the components of core values can result in a common organizational culture.

People deliver results.......Organizations grow.......Leaders succeed.

People	Organizations	Leadership
P – Passion	O – Opportunity	L - Listener
E – Energy	R – Relationships	E - Empathy
O – Openness	G – Growth	A - Authenticity
P – Partnerships	A – Acknowledgement	D - Development
L – Learners	N – Network	E - Ethics
E – Empowerment	I – Inspire	R – Respect
	Z - Zeal	S – Strategy
	A – Ambition	H – Humility
	T – Trust	I – Integrity
	I – Initiative	P – Pride
	O – Optimism	
	N – Nurturing	
	S – Spirit	

And, the values of authentic trust and passionate purpose are further reinforced by the compassion and empathy demonstrated by the leader.

> Take time to view a YouTube video from the Cleveland Clinical...
> ***Empathy: The Human Connection to Patient Care (2)***

Organizational Culture and Leadership

The human complexity and heart of an organization are created by a well-defined and implemented culture. This culture can drive employee engagement, builds successful productivity, and enhances a healthy work environment that evolves over time. It is aligned with values, behaviors and actions that are shaping the direction and future of the company.

There are three key questions that need to be examined to gain further insights into the culture, leadership, and *human chemistry* of the organization.

1. What defines the company culture and how is it created?

2. What connects culture to leadership behaviors?

3. What are the qualities of a high-performance culture?

Defining and Creating an Organizational Culture

People, from leaders and peers, to employees and co-workers, are the creators and drivers of cultures based on their beliefs, attitudes, and values. It is the human perceptions and interactions that shape acceptable behaviors and practices. They actually become the foundation for the alignment of the culture with the organizational values as well as with the company vision and mission. Through a dynamic culture, trust and respect develops and evolves along with a healthy work environment. Employees are engaged with each other and are positively connected to their work as well as team members. They live by the defined values and communicate openly from the heart. Happy employees find their work meaningful and they grow from praise along with outward recognition.

People with positive behaviors create positive relationships. Employees of an organization that feel consistently supported and appreciated as they are growing and enhancing their skills and abilities, are more likely to contribute constructively to the successes of the company. This type of mindset becomes the norm. A caring as well as empowering workplace builds employee loyalty, helps retain valued employees, and can serve as a way to attract future talent. The culture is shaped by the engaging actions of leaders, teams, and employees, all fostering organizational connections that are strategic in nature have clear purpose. The outcome of a well-defined culture is a company made up of people with emotional and personal commitments, and a workforce with a strong desire to perform and add to the organization's future.

Culture and Leadership Behaviors

Leaders are the drivers and enhancers of creative as well as productive work cultures. They encourage the focus on and the embracement of the core values, and they have the ability to influence the attitudes and behaviors of the employee population. Even though that leaders have the responsibility to be organizational strategists, they must be fully involved in the evolution of the workplace culture. They need to recognize and accept the importance of promoting collaboration and open communication. Their own personal behaviors and actions may build the cultural ideology and the core values. Yes, leaders are always committed to many business factors such as to analyzing business opportunities, to driving organizational goals and objectives, to properly allocating resources, and to acknowledging and rewarding accomplishment. Leaders are growing and securing the culture through their demonstrated openness, authenticity, and inclusion. Their compassionate approaches to challenges and clear perspectives to problems, along with a passionate interest in the employee population, can all truly impacts the culture of the organization as well as the potential of accomplishing the company vision.

Qualities of a High-Performance Culture

A quality focused culture is built on several elements, such as a compelling company vision, realistic and inspiring leadership, and values that are shared by all employees. The expected behaviors and attitudes need to be fully infused throughout the employee population, and performance metrics need to be clearly defined as well as connected to the company mission and direction. Successful and quality driven organizations have strong financial performance and are able to demonstrate a high level of agility and flexibility with changing global markets. Communication is open and active listening at all levels has become the norm. Healthy employee relationships exist and grow because of personal inclusion and collaboration. A very supportive work environment will drive, inspire and build higher levels of creativity, accountability, and commitment. And interestingly, happiness becomes pervasive in a well-run organization with its high-performance, quality-focused culture.

The Personal Stories

Story One - Values from Childhood into Adulthood

Values are the foundation for life in that they establish personal behaviors and beliefs. They define an individual specific to relationships, partnerships, and friendships. They can impact the approaches to addressing challenges, to communicating and connecting with others, to personal growth and development, and to building trust and integrity. My parents were loving individuals, always focused on enhancing a positive family environment. They encouraged levels of creativity, risk taking, and a desire to make inner discoveries. Things like music, family dinners, vacations together, and church participation, all influenced our appreciation of others, the need to be polite and respectful, and the value of demonstrating and sharing kindness.

My father, unfortunately, passed away of a heart attack on my 25th birthday. He was a man who was very dedicated to his family, his business, and to his friendships. He was always very supportive of family and others in his vast community of relationships. He encouraged his five sons to constantly try new things and explore, driving a focus on finding internal and emotional creativity. I love to this day building and utilizing the special skill of crafting imagination into reality via execution. Throughout our 44 years of marriage, my wife and I have together renovated two old homes – one built in 1901, and the other in 1908. We have found tremendous enjoyment in the creation of "environments", and even in the enhancement of a new home with carefully selected antiques, structure, and color. My father instilled in me the value and importance of having a free and open mind to create and develop a future, both physically and emotionally. My mother also drove within me values associated with kindness and appreciation, as well as the importance of finding happiness and fun in all relationships. My wife and I, based on both of our family connections and love, were able to build key values and meaning into the lives of our two wonderful children. Clearly, family values and beliefs have helped shape my behaviors and attitudes for life, and to define my personal leadership competencies utilized throughout my teaching and business worlds.

Story Two - A Reflective Note from my daughter

Renee found an old notebook/journal while cleaning out decades of paperwork and consolidating documents. She sent me the two pages that she had written during a flight to South Caroline for a job interview – mid 2000s. ((Parents infuse values and a family-oriented culture into their children based on their own integrity, love, courage, and wisdom….I think!))

Dad,

I just want to thank you for all of the valuable lessons that I have learned from you. In each and every interview, my thoughts are always "what would dad think is the right response…..?" to each question. I think I did very well with the interviews, and it was a nice trip.

I also think that my anxiety is very much under control. All I do is sleep on the planes without a care. It's all good. I am sitting in the Detroit airport right now. Long layover. On a totally different note, I know I have caused you and mom a lot of stress over the past several years. I am sorry for that, but I think we have all benefited from those experiences. And, life goes on. I am so happy that you and mom moved to New York and down-scaled. I am certain you will be very happy in that house. You and mom will always be my best friends. We need to mesh our lives together some more. I really enjoy being with you. Well, I've got to eat my steak quesadillas.....

Love, Renee

Story Three - Core Values, Culture, and the Getinge Group

During 2009 / 2010, the Getinge Group in Sweden, a global medical device corporation, carefully defined four company core values, established eight key leadership competencies, and built a value champion development program. All components of these three initiatives evolved over time and grew into new structures under new leadership. An examination of the approaches to all aspects of the three activities can provide many insights into the formation of organizational values, leadership competencies, and company culture along with continued focus on world class excellence.

The overall goal of the Getinge Group was to establish the company's core values and to build a unified common culture. The primary challenge was to take into account the dynamics of a global, internationalized organization located in many countries around the world. There were issues of local influences, different management communication styles, and leadership approaches based on varied business backgrounds. There were different social customs and levels of risk taking, potentially effecting creativity and innovation. There was a special need to be fully aware of the initiative processes being utilized to provide constant clarity – trying not to slow down the development and communication of the core values by adding levels of bureaucracy. It was a well understood that the culture would evolve and define itself over time.

Many factors were taken into account.

- To get many individuals involved and engaged in the process – at all steps along the way, from brainstorming and development, to implementation.
- To always be focused, clear and not ambiguous with the desired values.
- To show flexibility and openness, and to communicate constantly about the initiative.
- To make the core values unique so that they could meet employee needs globally, at all levels and positions.
- And, to demonstrate the impact of the values on actions and behaviors in all practices of the businesses, such as hiring and promotions.

The initial four core values were to serve as guidance for both the organization's internal conduct as well as the relationships with the external customers, partners and suppliers. These values represented the constant in an ever-changing world. They were the foundation for work, interactions, and the strategies that were employed to fulfill the company mission. The four values served as the basic elements to guide business processes and decision-making practices. And, all employees were expected to act in accordance with these values and principles, as well as follow the laws and regulations that influenced the operational activities. The core values were ....

1. *Openness* – because trust is based on openness, and everyone within the company must be able to take responsibility for their actions as employees.

2. *Confidence* – because all customers, employees and other stakeholders must be able to feel totally confident in their respective relationships with the organization.

3. *Pride* – because proud, committed employees deliver quality, and proud employees perform even better on behalf of customers and other stakeholders.

4. *Sustainability* – because the corporation strives to contribute to the establishing of a sustainable society.

Besides the four core values, four "Cornerstones" were assembled to serve as the guiding principles and the foundational structure for the company leadership competencies. These cornerstones served as a way to develop a work atmosphere that was performance focused and encouraged creativity. It produced an atmosphere where employees are challenged and engaged in their work. There was a strong focus on continuous improvement and learning & development, so that employees would always seek what was best for the customer. The four Cornerstones were – Inspire Others / Take Initiative / Drive Innovation / Deliver Results.

Over time and new leadership, the Core Values evolved with a stronger focus on people and passion.

Collaboration – working together to encourage positive outcomes.

Openness – the foundation of a feedback culture respectfully listening to every contribution.

Excellence – a commitment to best-in-class products, people and processes.

Ownership – a proactive effort, being empowered to make important decisions.

The key discoveries, regardless of the selected core value and descriptions, was that the entire organization from top to bottom all lived and conducted their business activities in accordance with the company values. The values help drive the human connections and human presence. They became the guiding principles to building and driving successful business outcomes along with an engaged workforce.

Closing Remarks

Core values will vary from organization to organization. The company culture will constantly evolve over time. Yet, two components are always critical for success …………

> **Trust – *Authentic Trust and Compassionate Integrity* and Purpose – *Clear Purpose and a Passionate Vision***
>
> As per Stephen M.R. Covey, author of **The Speed of Trust** – *"Trust is the highest form of human motivation. It brings the very best in people."* (3)
>
> As per David Horsager, author of **The Trusted Edge – How Top Leaders Gain Faster Results, Deeper Relationships, and a Stronger Bottom Line** – *"Trust has become the world's most precious resource. Trust can accelerate and mistrust can destroy any business, organization, or relationship. The lower the trust, the more time everything takes, the more everything costs, and the lower the loyalty of everyone involved. By contrast, greater trust brings superior innovation, creativity, freedom, morale, and productivity."* (4)
>
> And as per Bill George, author of **True North** – *"Leaders can sustain their effectiveness only if they empower employees around a shared purpose. As a leader, you must convey passion for the business every day while maintaining clarity about the mission of your organization."* (5)

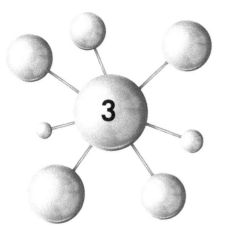

LEADERSHIP AND CRITICAL THINKING / COURAGE

Leaders as drivers of problem-solving, decision-making, and risk-taking.

The Chemistry Connection

On October 5, 1993, Leonard S. Kogut, professor of chemistry at Penn State, presented a paper entitled *Critical Thinking in General Chemistry* at the 25th Central Regional Meeting of the American Chemical Society, Pittsburgh, Pennsylvania. (1) He described how he discovered that first-year college chemistry students were "unskilled at critical thinking". He conducted several exercises, one using the noble gases of elements (He, Ne, Ar, Kr, Xe), and he asked his students to determine the number of protons and neutrons in the nucleus of each of the atoms, along with other questions. The students lacked the ability to analyze data and they were weak at practicing critical thinking. There was a need to conduct more classroom discussions and group problem-solving to be able to enhance the abilities to examine data and form valued hypotheses.

Leaders are always building inner self-awareness and critical thinking abilities. They are continuously enhancing their decision-making skills along with a focus on customer needs specific to change initiatives, and on setting strategic direction for the employee population. Leaders need to embrace the importance of taking risks and to having the courage to constructively explore critical business situations that go beyond the simple norms. They must constantly engage people throughout the organization and challenge data-details with thoughtful processes and approaches. Having a high level of personal and behavioral openness can lead to greater discoveries as well as outstanding managerial decisions. They become leaders with confidence and competence, capable of driving future organizational successes and outcomes. Without a doubt, leadership is a learning journey based on energetic growth and incredible *human chemistry*.

General Leadership Remarks

Leadership that is evolving into the future will be built on many soft skills and on the abilities to handle the challenges of a more complex workplace culture. Besides enhancing personal self-awareness and active communication capabilities, critical thinking is becoming an important leadership competency as well as intellectual discipline. There is a need for insightful analysis of situations and self-regulatory judgment. This thinking process will impact many leadership activities, such as problem-solving, decision-making, creative thinking, and reflective reasoning.

Leadership is a true growth-oriented learning journey. Building higher levels of risk-taking, being vulnerable, and enhancing inner courage, are all key components of the skill-sets of an effective and impactful leader. They must always show gratitude toward others and acknowledge business contributions. Leaders will need to communicate from their hearts with passion and to show compassion during difficult times. They will need to build diversity in the workforce, and to respectfully accept differences in beliefs as well as in strategic ideas. Leaders need to be strong, demonstrate confidence in their roles, and rise above all challenges with total professionalism as they face each-and-every day. They must find their inner creativity and have a deep level of imagination. And, most of all, they must always focus on people with reality and humbleness.

Critical Thinking and Leadership

Critical thinking is a real-life competency that is becoming more important for leaders in today's rapidly changing world. There is a higher requirement for flexibility and adaptability in understanding issues and challenges within the workplace. Leaders need to continue to build greater levels of personal self-awareness so that they will be able to balance their thoughts with their emotions. Critical thinking is a learned skill that should be integrated into all learning and development activities, such as strategy formulations, team leadership, and change management. It is the foundation for thinking out-side-of-the-box, along with more reflective approaches to leading others.

Leaders are learning to become more effective as well as efficient with problem-solving and decision-making. Critical thinking and conceptualizing along with skillful data analysis and information evaluation will help maximize the process of reaching successful conclusions and outcomes. By enhancing the ability to examine strengths and weaknesses in a problem, there is a higher possibility of finding alternative as well as diverse solutions. Leaders are always tackling new daily demands as they move into unknown territories of reasoning and logical thinking. Therefore, they must force themselves to think and apply ideas and decisive conclusions more systematically while being open-minded. Critical thinking can even help prevent big mistakes, yet not give up a leader's willingness to be vulnerable as well as be wrong some times.

The competency of critical thinking has tremendous value for a leader. By utilizing reasoning and thinking processes along with the involvement of the employee population, teamwork is fostered, and communications is enhanced. By looking for diversity of solutions and by getting different inputs along with new ideas and approaches, there clearly is an increase in the potential for positive and successful actions. The removal of conventional assumptions and a narrow focus on solutions, sounder decisions can be reached, even with a reduction in the time required for the decision. So, the system of critical thinking by leaders, using both inductive and deductive reasoning, can result in an outstanding impact on complex business accomplishments.

Problem-Solving, Decision-Making and Leadership

Leaders face regular challenges every day and are responsible for finding the best solutions to problems as they surface. All problems may vary based on a lack of clarity and have their own aspects of complexity. They can even become more difficult to address due to the potential constraints associated with the facts and circumstances. There are many techniques or methods that a leader can utilize in problem-solving, such as trial & error, brainstorming, root cause analysis, modeling, and others. Regardless, leaders develop steps to build their insights, expertise, and knowledge for reaching the ideal solutions. The upfront work on defining the problem is based on the gathering of the details and carefully observing the situation. This is followed by establishing a strategy, experimenting with the data, and implementing changes. Action are taken, and post-evaluations determine the success of the problem-solving flow of events.

Leaders need to understand the various barriers that will surface and how to tackle the many roadblocks that they will find on the path to the best solutions. Using past or conventional techniques may not be adequate or optimal, and new approaches may have to be applied. Imposing too many limitations can even cause a narrow focus, just as over using aspects of common sense can result in under thinking a possible solution. Group input may be beneficial, yet there is a tendency to get stuck on one solution usually based on over reliance of team thinking. Many times insights into problems get off track because of the use of irrelevant information. Leaders need to remain fully focused and motivated to find ideal conclusions to problems. They need to enhance the way they apply logic and rules along with their personal thoughts and information reasoning. They can look at "cause & effect" in separating out good choices from bad choices. They have to balance their intellectual reasoning from their "head" with their passion, feelings, and emotions from their "heart".

Leaders can drive successful decisions and effective results by making the best decisions from accurate assumptions and, as described earlier, by good problem-solving. They must have a strong commitment to being imaginative in the problem-solving / decision-making process. Leaders balance several factors along the pathway of reflection and discovery. They gain participation from others to find multiple perspectives and take enough time to be successful. They build enthusiasm toward group participation, encouraging debates, active listening, and open disclosure of options. This shared ownership for solutions can build respect and trust with all team players as well as with leaders. And, the leader must keep learning and finding new levels of being flexible in their decision activities and actions.

So, the outcome to decision-making is a custom-crafted solution with sound design and clear actions. Just as with problem-solving, the decision process follows specific steps – define / diagnose / analyze / act / test. These evaluation steps can be further described as follows:

1. Determine potential impact and critical importance of the decision.

2. Generate a detailed and comprehensive list of options.

3. Assess the key decision possibilities and establish a timeline for the decision process, always reviewing the pros and cons of the alternative choices.

4. Consider a team / group consensus decision and move forward.

5. Evaluate the decision and the process.

Once again, there is a need to balance several components throughout the decision-making activities – fast versus slow; risk versus reward; advantages versus disadvantages; complexity versus simplification; instinct versus logic; thoughts versus emotions (gut). Yes, successful and effective leaders are **critical thinkers.** They have learned the value of collective intelligence and the ability to recognize the need for additional information and facts. They show confidence, use good judgment, and are willing to accept mistakes, specific to short-term goals as well as long-term strategies. Leaders have learned from past experiences and have grown an open mindedness to new perspectives and new opportunities.

As per Henry Ford (1863 – 1947), American Industrialist and Founder of the Ford Motor Company, *"Most people spend more time and energy going around problems than in trying to solve them." (2)*

And, as per Grace Speare, Author, *"Welcome every problem as an opportunity. Each moment is the great challenge, the best thing that ever happened to you. The more difficult the problem, the greater the challenge in working it out." (3)*

Risk-taking, Courage, and Leadership

Making bold decisions and being innovative with non-traditional ideas and business approaches, takes risk and courage, especially by leaders as well as by all employees in the workplace. Being courageous and being willing to step out of a comfortable place can benefit the entire organization. And, yes, the courageous behaviors by leaders can be very inspiring and motivating for the employee population.

Great leaders build their environments and company cultures with colleagues based on establishing a well-defined vision and clear goals. They confidently find great ideas, confront issues by gaining support from others, and demonstrate a willingness to accept the need for change successfully. To become a risk-taking leader, there needs to be a spirit to practice courage regularly, to dare frequently, and to even break the rules every so often. There is also a need for self-disciple to move things forward and to implement actions. Choices are driven by actual perceived opportunities associated with the desired outcomes, the specific timing of the actual action, and the available details as well as knowledge of a situation. Risks can be reduced by looking back at past experiences as well as the analysis applied at that time, and by the examination of the business results, along with the financial investment made with the specific decision.

Similar to problem-solving and decision-making, the leader can take a step-by-step approach that can help minimize the risk and even provide room for personal growth and learning, especially when the choices may not be perfect or correct.

Step One is the gathering of the details and supportive information associated with the risk level of the opportunity.

- Defining the objective and its potential value helps diagnose the size of the risk.
- It provides clarity of the business choice.

Step Two is the gaining of a handle on the consequences of the risk-taking decision.

- A review of alternatives can provide insights into timing and the cost impact.
- Assessing assumptions can help minimize incorrect choices and negative outcomes.

Step Three is addressing barriers for success and actually taking the action.

- Miscalculations can sometimes result in potential failure.
- So, it is important for the leader not to be always overly optimistic or even, impulsive.

Taking each step requires disciple as well as courage, guts and grit, along with personal tenacity. Moving out of the comfort zone can be a learning experience for a leader since it will build new strengths and energize higher levels of flexibility, creativity, and imagination. Fear is the biggest limiting factor that can inhibit leadership performance. The unknown along with the potential for failure creates levels of dysfunctionality and reduces general engagement. Having courage and asserting risk-oriented judgment is an important component for the leader and for the business. It demonstrates confidence to take initiatives, to handle change, and to build trust with the employee population. Difficult and risky decisions need to be made with decisiveness as well as with inclusion. Courageous leaders rise above their fears and use these challenges as competitive advantages. They can help motivate others and gain commitment to new solutions for the implementation of actions. The vulnerability of the leader and their personal accountability can lead to growth and to the achievement of more aggressive organizational strategies.

Becoming a courageous leader is based on emotional intelligence and on having moral courage, the willingness to stand-up for what one believes is right. These are leaders with curiosity and with a willingness to ask questions that show interest in other ideas and approaches to problems. They are leaders with empathy, challenging decisions and even being contradictory at times. Regardless of fear and discomfort, risk-taking initiatives are done with a high degree of passion and self-esteem. Clearly, there are always external influencing factors, such as economic turbulence, indirect and direct competition, and even employee disagreements. Regardless, courage demonstrates confidence, and confidence builds trust.

Here are two simple "examples" based on trust that drives home the point of confidence and risk.

> There is a farm stand that is along the side of the road in the country. The fantastic vegetables and fruits are carefully displayed, and simple signs define the pricing per item. Bags are provided for the visitors. A friendly sign states – "Leave the cash amount. Enjoy the fresh and great tasting items". *Trust and confidence are part of the risk!*

There is a coffee cart vendor on a street in New York City that demonstrates a focus by the owner on the customers. The cup of coffee is prepared as per the request, cost is shared, and the "correct" amount is left on the cart shelf – some customers leaving more, and maybe some leaving less. The key is that all customers receive their coffees very quickly and successfully, without a focus on money. Again, *trust and confidence are part of the risk!*

The Personal Stories - Self-Reflection and Self-Discovery

Story #1 - My leadership learning journey from college to retirement

In 1969, I graduated from Wagner College, located on Staten Island, New York, with a degree in chemistry along with many learning memories. I was full of energy and enthusiasm, and had an exceptional passion for life as well as a strong desire to have a productive and rewarding career. Now in retirement, I have discovered that life is a true learning journey. It all starts during childhood based on the major influences of parents and siblings, specific to values and a family-oriented culture. My parents were German immigrants with very clear core values specific to integrity, humility and empathy. They encouraged high levels of openness and always showed a willingness to help all five sons find their inner generosity, love, and wisdom. Besides enhancing our courage and conviction, they created principles based on respect. My brothers, one being an identical twin brother, all pursued very diverse careers, from business and music, to medicine and film production. Yet, a key step in my personal growth was attending college, exploring my independence, and building self-awareness. As a college freshman away from family, I was no longer seen as a twin, but rather as an individual focused on my relationships and my personal pursuit of opportunities.

Reflecting back, college served as the foundation for the learning of many leadership competencies and skills. These capabilities and behaviors became critical components and success factors throughout my diverse teaching and business career. They defined my personal identity such as my sense of humor, my passion to learn, my exceptional level of energy, my strong commitment to life, and my clearly established values. They helped enhance other individual aspects such as creativity, imagination, and a willingness to take risks. College was a time for self-discovery, fun, and, of course, hard work.

The four years of undergraduate studies at Wagner were full of many engaging interactions and experiences. Here are three simple memories:

> The professors all had different teaching styles. The Professor of Organic Chemistry, lectured and wrote formulas on the board with the chalk in one hand, and an eraser in the other. I learned quickly how to capture notes at high speed.

> I had a lab partner, Emily, for all four years at Wagner. She was a very friendly individual, and was willing to tolerate my behaviors of arriving late and being silly. I learned the importance of communication and active listening, as well as the value of building relationships and teamwork.

> I was required to take one semester of Scientific German and the final exam was a challenging experience – translating a page in German from a science publication into English. Some of the words went across the entire page. I proceeded to write a "story" based on words that I could translate and attempted to build a picture of a scientific investigation. The

professor passed me based on my "creative and imaginative translation".

All of the learning activities at Wagner became part of my different management and leadership approaches. And, my personal connecting style evolved throughout my career based on exceptional experiences, engaging relationships, and fantastic discoveries along the daily pathway.

General Reflections

My career followed several revolutionary steps - from teaching high school chemistry for ten years, to a marketing role for a chemical company. I eventually moved into human resource management, followed by several vice president positions focused on global learning and development, employee engagement, company branding, and executive coaching. Throughout my career, I continued my education, completing my first masters at Wagner, and a second masters in management at Stevens Institute of Technology. I continued to grow and develop my skills, insights, and competencies by doing post graduate programs at University of Pennsylvania, Cornell University, University of Southern California, Harvard Law, and even Copenhagen Business School. I made additional personal self-discoveries by gaining my coaching certification at the Hudson Institute of Santa Barbara, and have always been on a life learning journey. I retired a few years ago, established a leadership consulting practice, and write articles every month.

Story #2 – Teaching Chemistry

Looking back to the years that I taught chemistry, I developed and utilized the leadership competency of influencing others. In the classroom, the teacher serves as the catalyst, sparking the learning of the subject content and igniting the potential of applying new and exciting concepts. The students master the uniqueness of both physical and chemical properties through their involvement and sharing of thoughts as well as imposing questions. As a teacher and as a leader, I have learned the importance that authentic communicating and influencing of actions and commitments of others must come from the heart.

Throughout my career, I have discovered that leadership is more than just a science, more than just an art, and more than just a craft. Leadership is founded on *human chemistry* – the ability for a leader to look inward and to become fully self-aware, and the ability for a leader to look outward and to build an understanding of others. Specifically, leaders must meet the needs of people. They need to focus not on themselves, but on others. Leaders need to communicate openly, listen more, be honest with the facts, have a clear and inspiring vision, and be accountable for their actions. Leaders also must be compassionate and empathetic, and able to use both emotional and social intelligence to build relationships. Every leader has their own personal "chemistry" associated with their behaviors, thinking dynamics, managerial actions, performance approaches, and ways of connecting with people.

Story #3 – Business Decision-Making and an Engagement Survey

Following the corporate commitment to proceed with the execution of an employee engagement survey for the entire global organization, one of the critical steps in the decision-making activities was the selection of a consulting company. This group would provide the administrative support and the tools to design, launch, assess data, and communicate findings along with the implementation of actions. Key was to find the best resource to build this engagement survey and to drive all of the processes.

The careful assessment and selection of several consulting firms was based on specific criteria.

Step One – The identification of the support source along with the required resource people. Initially, several companies were selected for further review, and eventually narrowed down to three consulting organizations. General reviews were conducted specific to years of experience, global reach, client relationships, and special areas of expertise.

- The final three were: Towers Watson – UK; Netsurvey AB – Stockholm, Sweden; and Kenexa/IBM – US.
- Others that were looked at were: Success Factors/An SAP Company – California; ISR-Independent Strategic Research – London, UK; CLC Genesee – Corporate Leadership Council – US; Pilat Europe/North America – UK/New Jersey; and the University of Glasgow.

Based on the many conversations with these organizations, much was learned about the employee engagement survey process and the required commitment. This initiative was to provide insights into understanding manageable factors that caused people (employees) to work harder in their jobs, stay longer with the company, and to care more about their roles as well as colleagues. The engagement survey was to be viewed as a change management "tool" that could drive positive organizational outcomes and impact financial performance.

Step Two – Working more closely with the three selected firms, the project scope was further defined based on our company requirements and expectations. This served as the foundation to securing proposals specific to fees and optional service. The decision-process pathway gained focus.

- Besides reviewing the complete global network of the survey company and past experiences, additional selection criteria was established.

  - Survey design & structure as well as technology capabilities
  - Translation capabilities
  - Project management abilities and educational services
  - General philosophy and pricing

Step Three – The selection decision of the survey support company was carefully made and the business initiative was underway. Several success factors were defined to drive the process.

1. Top management commitment to the process

2. Strong prioritization and implementation of specific actions

3. Time and resources to support and drive changes

4. Open and regular communication

5. Recognition of the implemented changes

6. Monitoring and measuring of the change initiatives

A successful employee engagement survey was based on the initial selection decision-process followed by great implementation support. Four specific deployment activities occurred over several months.

A. Planning & Survey Design – communication / launch

B. Data Collection – administration / data gathering

C. Process & Analysis – discoveries / report generation

D. Results into Actions – feedback / manager training and action planning

The success of the employee engagement survey activities and actions were based on carefully made decisions, some levels of risk, and well-defined business outcomes.

Closing Remarks

Leadership is about using the head and the heart. It is about motivating employees and gaining their commitment to drive business performance and to address the accelerated pace of change. Wise leaders are constantly growing, evolving, and developing creative thinking capabilities and competencies throughout their journey. I have personally learned to develop my abilities to engage, not control others, to gain regular and constructive feedback, and to have a passion to drive corporate successes.

My leadership wisdom is based on experiences and knowledge throughout life. This wisdom has had an impact on my judgments, decisions, and actions. I have learned to always have a clear purpose and mission. My wisdom is founded on actively listening, on building engaging relationships, and on communicating with high levels of authenticity and clarity.

Yes, leadership is a learning journey with new competencies as well as enhanced capabilities that are developed and grown along the way. Having great self-awareness can help leaders achieve outstanding results. And using problem-solving and decision-making processes along with critical thinking and risk-taking can build personal trust, credibility, and confidence.

Courage demonstrates confidence, and confidence builds trust.

Leaders use their incredible *human chemistry* to be fully focused on people as people, to create outstandingly successful organizations, and to achieve fantastic accomplishments.

LEADERSHIP AND AUTHENTIC INFLUENCING SKILLS / EMOTIONAL INTELLIGENCE

Leaders using the power to change the thinking of people and their behaviors.

The Chemistry Connection

Active metals (elements), such as lithium (Li), sodium (Na) and potassium (K), react with "vigor" when they come into contact with water. This is a chemical reaction that converts substances or reactants into other products. Bonds are broken and atoms are rearranged. With active metals, hydrogen is displaced from water. Lithium reacts slowly, sodium reacts rapidly, and potassium reacts somewhat violently. The actual outcome is the production of metal hydroxide and hydrogen gas.

Similarly, a teacher works with its students and influences their learning through highly engaging reactions. Utilizing collaborative educational technics and discussions, students make discoveries and find learning and performance insights. Teachers are outstanding information imparters and connectors with their students. And, teachers as leaders are active listeners and authentic influencing communicators. Both, teachers and leaders help others grow as individuals and develop knowledge through various levels of "reactions" and "interactions", some slow and others, fast.

General Remarks on Leadership

Leadership is based on the ability to impact an organization in an inspiring way. It is the capability to drive extraordinary results as well as business outcomes by influencing the minds and hearts of the entire employee population. It is more than an art, a science, and a craft. Leadership is based on *human chemistry* – the ability to be fully self-aware, compassionate, and intellectually connected in all relationship. There is also an emotional component to leading and influencing colleagues and their co-workers. Yet, all leaders have different leadership styles specific to their individual ambitions and competencies, their level of innovative creativity, and their personal behavioral courage. And, each leader has a preferred style to influence other individuals. They may even alter this personal leadership approach specific to the changing organizational requirements and challenges.

Leaders as Authentic Influencers

Being an authentic influencing leader takes conviction and personal inner passion to be able to gain employee commitment and to create high levels of engagement. The skill of influencing is similar to several of the other leadership competencies, yet it is important enough to call it out as a specific value-oriented leadership characteristic. It is a way of developing followers that are empowered to be leaders themselves, and these individuals can become skilled relationship builders and drivers of business performance. Effective leaders are continuously growing and evolving their own personal strengths as well as supporting the development of all employees. These leaders are maximizing the capabilities of their teams to help enhance employee engagement with the organization and with the defined goals as well as mission. Basically, the authentic influencing leader is able to create influencing followers, individuals that take charge, speak up, and make sure that the vision and direction of the company are "heard" both internally and externally.

> As per Antoine de Saint-Exupery, a French aristocrat, writer, poet and pioneering aviator who lived between 1900 and 1944.....

> "If you want to build a ship, don't drum up people to collect wood and don't assign them tasks and work, but rather teach them to long for the endless immensity of the sea." (1)

So, what are some of the key resulting outcomes and values of being an influencing leader?

- Higher levels of engagement that drives organizational results.
- Creation of an environment that helps build critical thinking.
- Willingness of employees to move out of their comfort zones and to take risks.
- Enhancement and improvement of self-confidence, commitment, and loyalty.
- Stronger feeling of appreciation for contributions by working with an authentic leader.

To be an authentic and impactful influencing leader, they must have characteristics that are unique and genuine in nature. They may even have special aspects of being engaging as well as charismatic in their general make up and communication style. These leaders are highly respected and even admired by many, and have driving qualities that enable others to achieve the defined business objectives.

Leadership influencing qualities are based on the ability of the leader ...

... to earn respect

... to gain perspective by others in a positive way

... to find personal confidence in oneself

... to build ownership and competent control

... to enhance a desirable image

... to drive high standards and disciplined principles

... to energize a strong focus on performance and results

The leadership competency of influencing is built on collaboration with the employee population and the customer base. It is composed of both hard and soft skills and abilities of an individual. The hard skills are specifically based on the experiences and knowledge of the leaders used to develop strategic business plans and corporate direction. The soft skills serve as the foundation for inspiring communications throughout the organization as well as with external customers. Each leader masters many influencing skills with a range of effectiveness and with an ability to develop presence along with their personal individual identity. Yet, there are two competency areas that can have the greatest impact – an **assertive approach** to communicating and connecting, and an **interactive approach** to building alliances.

An effective assertive leader is not necessarily an aggressive communicator. They can influence others based on self-confidence and a willingness to share opinions and feelings in an open fashion. Assertive communication is usually respectful and non-judgmental in nature and, influencing with an interactive approach that is being an interactive leader, helps enhance two-way communication and the understanding of information specific to issues of concern. Healthy relationships can grow through the use of the soft components of connecting and via higher levels of personal awareness. Leadership is about influencing, directing and guiding of others with clear and inspirational organizational expectations and goals.

Assertive Approach

Wilson Learning Social Style Matrix Model (2) defines the human behavioral dimension of assertiveness as the *"way in which a person is perceived as attempting to influence the thoughts and actions of others"*. All leaders have a combination of "ask-directed" assertiveness and "tell-directed" assertiveness. By being more tell-oriented, the leader is very direct and firm in their communications, making declarative statements and using voice inflections to enhance areas of emphasis. The actual position on the assertiveness continuum depends on the organizational situations and on specific current business requirements. An assertive leader demonstrates strong judgement along with a clear purpose and direction, even when there are some levels of opposition and resistance. Assertive influencing of others, therefore, is a skill based on authority and decision-making, and also on demonstrating personal confidence and assurance. Strong gestures, facial expressions, and body language are utilized throughout the influencing conversational activities.

Interactive Approach

An interactive influencing leader is a strong negotiator as well as an individual that can successfully build consensus. These leaders are able to enlist the support and assistance from others, driving a cooperative environment that is based on a unified sense of purpose. Creative solutions and clear direction are always the results of key business decisions, building harmony and agreement with the organizational population and other leader individuals. These authentic and interactive influencing leaders are skilled at coaching and mentoring, as well as developing the abilities of employees so that they can be strong contributors to the company. And, there is a natural growth of valuable relationships and partnerships, along with positive personal connections.

Other Approaches

There are other influencing skills that are also important, yet they may have less impact. Examples such as convincing / persuasive communication abilities, and interpersonal skills are two attributes that demonstrate the energy, enthusiasm and commitment of an authentic influencing leader. Both of these capabilities help build connections, collaboration, and engagement. And, the result of these stimulating interactions and innovative problem-solving activities can even enhance emotional companionship. Therefore, all influencing skills are critical in driving company actions and results. Yet, assertive and interactive influencing competencies are key for successful business accomplishments and outcomes.

The Authentic Influencer Continuum
Going from Ask-Assertiveness--------------------To Tell-Assertiveness

Being more......		Being more.......
Authoritative	Strong Judgement	Direct
Gestures	Clear Purpose	Firm
Body Language	Negotiator	Declarative
Consensus Builder	Harmony	Persuasive
Coaching	Interpersonal	Results Driver
	Emotional	

So, what makes an authentic influencing leader effective in their role?

It is the achievement of a balanced focus in four capability areas:

➢ Area A

- o Having interpersonal strengths and self-confidence
- o Have social skills and empathy
- o Having a willingness not to accept the status quo

➢ Area B

- o Having the ability to maintain composure during uncertainty
- o Having a focus on trust and respect
- o Having the ability to communicate and negotiate openly
- o Having a handle on stress and tension
- o Having plans and clear vision

➢ Area C

- o Having an ability to recognize accomplishments
- o Having a focus on showing appreciation for contributions
- o Having a support for team involvement

➢ Area D

- o Having a driver of actions and implementation
- o Having an acceptance of personal vulnerability
- o Having a self-awareness and self-regularity of emotions

Leaders and Emotional Intelligence

Being an effective leader and authentic influencer can be connected back to the emotional intelligence of an individual. The EI personal component clearly affects how a leader manages others, navigates social complexities, and makes decision that drive positive results and strong business successes. The EI will impact the behaviors that may have an intangible nature to them, and it can influence everything a leader does and says. The emotional component of influencing and leading is driven by the personal self-awareness of the leader. It is a special ability to be fully aware of one's own emotions as well as the emotions in other people, and it serves as an outstanding connection to what is going on within the employee population. Human behaviors are an essential part of the whole person. Emotional intelligence, without a doubt, can drive the professional successes of the leader, such as the skill to authentically influencing individuals. And yes, other competencies such as decision-making, utilizing empathy, time management, and trust building, are all connected to emotional intelligence.

Transforming organizational cultures and impacting company interactive engagements are driven by the behaviors of leaders and their abilities to demonstrate aspects of caring with an open heart that is anchored on authenticity and humility. Through the connection of leaders to their emotional intelligence, four specific areas are utilized and grown.

1. *Building relationships and influencing others.*

    Leaders that are good listeners, networkers, and inspirers, have a great handle on their emotional intelligence to assemble desirable goals and to focus on specific organizational needs. Conflicts are carefully managed, and change initiatives are driven by the assembly of a common purpose.

2. *Finding insights through self-awareness.*

   Leaders use emotional self-awareness and a powerful handle on personal feelings to drive business and
   people performance. Their self-confidence can enhance
   outcomes along with a higher level of employee engagement and organizational presence.

3. *Driving achievement through the management of different leadership styles.*

   Leaders have different emotional internal structures and
   intelligence make-up. They need to have a willingness to
   be adaptive to organizational challenges and business
   ambiguities. Different leadership styles will have different approaches to problem-solving as well as to methods of connecting with colleagues. Yet, through the
   transparent behaviors of leaders, company needs and
   demands can be fully addressed and driven so that opportunities are handled optimistically and successfully.

4. *Enhancing organizational awareness.*

   Leaders must manage political forces and help the total employee population focus on the company mission
   and on the established values. Again, the emotional intelligence of a leader enhances relationships and provides a connection with empathy for people. Leaders
   constantly gain new perspectives and continually grow
   their presence throughout the organization.

So, influencing interactive behavioral skills and emotional intelligence are soft leadership competencies. They impact communication and interactions by specifically utilizing to effective questioning
as well as active listening. Even though emotional intelligence may
have somewhat intangible factors, it serves as the foundation for

socially connecting behaviors. Leaders are clearly change agents that have learned how to balance professional and personal elements within their lives. The strength of influencing can serve as the basis for finding new solutions to issues and to discovering new possibilities to challenging organizational strategies. Ultimately, the capability of persuasive communication builds leadership engagement along with an exciting company message, and a passion for the business.

Authentic Influencing Skills and Emotional Intelligence

Personal Story #1 – Teaching

With a high level of enthusiasm and commitment, early September 1970, I had the great privilege to assume the role of a classroom chemistry teacher at Summit High School in Summit, New Jersey. I was only six or seven years older than the students that I would be influencing and teaching. I held a BS degree in chemistry as well as the strong confidence and desire to be a classroom "educator-performer". I had taught biology for three months during the Spring of 1970 in another school district as a perdeim teacher, following a learning experience at University of Pennsylvania during the Fall 1969.

Reflecting back on my ten-year teaching "experience" at Summit High School, I have made many personal discoveries specific to the teaching world and the influencing environment. There were three key components associated with this self-reflective and self-discovery process.

One

Teacher effectiveness was built and driven by the desire of the students to want to be part of the classroom activities. They had a passion and a willingness to challenge concepts and aspects of the chemistry course content. The students had strong needs to participate and learn as well as have fun, by always finding value in the classroom teacher-student interactions and relationships.

Two

My instructional methodology and approaches to learning may have been unconventional at times, yet all material content was covered flawlessly. Students understood the consequences associated with the participation and learning of the subject matter, yet they always felt well supported, and appreciated an authentic and active-listening teacher.

Three

Learning objectives were carefully defined, clearly focused on, and specifically driven. As an influencing teacher - courage, openness, and honesty, as well as a sense of humor - all helped establish the foundation for an engaging and interactive classroom experience. Even though as the teacher, not always having the answers to some questions, a process was created to gain additional insights and understanding of concepts. Both student and teacher needed to research and find a possible solution to the question. It was shared the following day. This discovery approach-built ownership in the learning process and drove the most successful learning experiences for the entire class.

Personal Story #2 - Engaging Teaching and Influencing

The success of an engaging and connected learning environment was based on TLC – "Tender-Loving-Care". Yet, the TLC in my teaching world was defined by three different pieces – the "T" for teacher; the "L" for learning; and the "C" for the chemistry curriculum. The classroom environment establishes the stage for thinking, challenging, discovering, and learning. Through the sharing of insights and ideas openly, knowledge and talent were developed, along with the growth of interpersonal relationships. Through the experiences in lab-work and student partnerships, realistic interactions were enhanced and innovative problem-solving become the norm.

"T"

As the teacher, I served as the agent for providing the knowledge of chemistry. My influencing successes were based on my ability to connect with the students and to form a type of emotional companionship. I was young, cool (I think), and down to earth with my content communication and stories. I made the learning experience challenging and interesting as well as fun.

"L"

The learners were the students of chemistry. Actually, I was also a learner as we were growing and discovering concepts and communication approaches together. Our open and honest sharing of insights helped build and motivate authentic emotions and new perspectives on life as well as on technological thinking.

"C"

The curriculum of the chemistry course being taught was well-defined and based on a well-structured text book. The program had clear objectives, strong and in-depth content, and excellent tactical flow.

Teaching truly utilizes the leadership competency of influencing. It is a way of impacting engaging relationships and emotional connections to the life-long learning journey. In the world of chemistry, the teacher serves as the catalyst, sparking the learning of the subject content and igniting the potential of applying new and exciting concepts. The students master the uniqueness of both physical and chemical properties through their involvement and sharing of thoughts as well as imposing challenging questions. The classroom fosters and energizes collaboration, listening, and absorbing of ideas and concepts. New skills and knowledge are developed along with the growth of personal emotional intelligence. Learning is based on a discovery process and on building diverse perspectives in life.

Personal Story #3 - More on the personal side

The personal experiences as a chemistry teacher have led to my broad development of being an impactful influencer, growing my emotional intelligence and enhancing my effective leadership competencies. And, these capabilities became critical components in my many business leadership roles and management activities that occurred throughout my fantastic career.

Here are some of the specific learnings and accomplishments that occurred during this high school teaching period of my career. I believe that I was a very real, authentic, and fun-loving teacher. My successes were based on my passion as well as commitment to teaching effectively, and my ability to get students to actually think constructively. I fully enjoyed being in the classroom environment and in finding new ways of reaching student learning needs. Even though I initially did not have my teaching certification (yet achieved via my first master's degree within three years), I had the enthusiasm, perseverance, and ability to perform and influence my chemistry "learners" and to impact their growth. And, throughout this first stage of my career, I also had the full support of my family, wife and children.

The Grading Story – A Second Chance

At the close of each of the first quarters of the school year, I would review with each student, on a one-on-one basis, their academic accomplishments specific to test scores and lab report achievements. Unfortunately, there was a handful of students that had weak grades and actually representing failure for the quarter. Following a careful review of their lack of success, I indicated a willingness to pass them this one time by giving them a "D minus", versus the "big F". They were appreciative and indicated that parental punishment would be minimized. This act of kindness provided these unsuccessful students with a new level of motivation, usually resulting in 9-out-of-10 students raising their grades during the following subsequent three quarters. They had a new level of commitment and desire to improve and succeed based on my willingness to give them a second chance.

The Classroom Content Question Story

As expected, students continuously asked subject questions and engaged in the chemistry content. Occasionally, as described earlier, I did not have the full explanation or answer to the chemistry issue. So, we committed to the following process – both the teacher and the student would go home and research the question. Our findings would be shared and compared during the next classroom gathering. The student was proud of their discoveries and very happy to share their findings with their classmates. Influencing their personal involvement enhanced the learning experience for all.

The Letter Grading System Story

Many students did not like the overly structured and focused approach to grading for test achievements and lab reporting accomplishments. There was too much attention on the "As, Bs, Cs" versus the learnings. Yet, the students could not come up with an alternative approach other than "no grades". So, I recommended a system specific to "achievement points". All grading and scoring was based on 25 points per test or report. Yes, for example, 20 points multiplied by four equals 80 or the letter grade of "B". There was a shift to a focus on gathering points based on learning successes versus a grade. The desire to learn, understand content, apply concepts, and achieve results became more critically important than an actual letter grade.

The Classroom Structure Story

Based on the general school expectations, the classroom chairs/desks were aligned in row. This was clearly a functional structure that provided some student separation, and also pathways for "walking connections and engaging influencing". I found myself walking and sitting among the students versus standing behind the demonstration counter in the front of the classroom. Face-to-face interactions, listening actively, coaching and asking challenging questions became the norm. Interestingly, during the taking of tests, students learned that looking at their neighbor's paper could result in the other student's failure. Therefore, everyone protected their documents and cheating was never an issue.

The Chemistry Demonstration Story

To drive home various chemistry learning points, "performance demonstration" methods were used. The intention was to influence and enhance the learning. Here are three examples that I personally enjoyed "performing".

1. Rates of reactions – Using an organic spore, lycopodium, and lighting it on fire with a Bunsen burner, and agitating the small pile, resulted in a greater size flame. An increase in surface area increased the rate of reaction. Very easy to

see and understand. The surprise came during the clean-up of the demo and my dumping of the remaining pile into the garbage can. The spore pile fire had not been extinguished properly and massive flames shot from the waste can. Unexpectedly, even greater surface area had been created. An outstanding, exciting, and, surprisingly, learning experience was achieved and used each year thereafter.

2. Active metal in water (as described at the beginning of the chapter) – rather than using a small beaker with an inch of water (reaction containment) to produce a small hydrogen "pop", it was more dramatic to pitch a larger chunk of the chemical element into the lab sink on the other side of the room that had 4 inches of water at the bottom. Results – a much more dramatic explosive reaction. Clearly, another very memorable demo experience that drove home the learning points by a "performer".

3. Periodic Table of Elements review – Rather than just pointing at the elements and the data of the large chart hanging on the side of the classroom, I personally stood behind the wall chart that I pulled down in front of me. From behind, I verbally let the Periodic Table of Elements come "alive" as I described all aspects of this key chemistry tool. The students looked and listened with amazement, and were fully engaged in the learning event. Yes, leadership and learning can be fun.

General Summary on Leadership and Authentic Influencing

Leadership is a learning journey based on *human chemistry.* Leaders are continuously learning to be strong observers, emotionally engaged individuals, and realistic influencer of the actions and commitments of others. They take risks and have a passion for creative and positive outcomes. Teachers are outstanding knowledge imparters, connectors, active listeners, and authentic communicators. Both leaders and teachers help others grow and develop their knowledge and competencies, always doing the building of strengths from the heart, and always showing the complete appreciation for accomplishments and contributions.

So, *strong and effective leaders*, *authentic influencers*, and *interactive teachers*............

- Have a way to connect their work with all components of life.
- Have clear direction, expectations and purpose.
- Have a strong focus on people and students.
- Have a handle on their primary and secondary leadership styles.
- Have a great ability to build dynamic and reflective relationships.
- Have a capability to add value by making selective decisions and delegation.

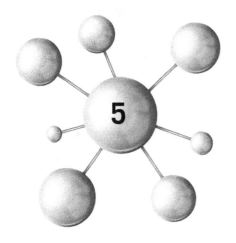

LEADERSHIP AND DYNAMIC RELATIONSHIPS

Leaders building connections with employees, teams, and customers.

The Chemistry Connection

Two separate molecules – oxygen (O_2) and hydrogen (H_2), both having very different chemical properties, can "unit" together and combine into a very new and different, yet well-known substance called water (H_2O). Each piece of the molecular structure participates and works together based on their bonds with each other and on their different levels of molecular weight. Interestingly, two hydrogen atoms are 11% of the water molecule, and one oxygen atom is 89% of the compound.

Leadership is one of the critical components for engaging, building, and maintaining internal and external business relationships. The personal connections drive the people interactions specific to *human chemistry*. The collaboration of motivated groups and teams join or "bond" their energies and capabilities to enhance organizational cultures and business outcomes. And, leaders need to encourage strong contributions, to secure continuous input, and to share information from all individuals through their relationships with each other within the work environment. These connections and partnerships are the drivers of successful accomplishments and results, and they are further supported by employee diversities and their past business experiences.

> *(For fun – view a video on YouTub – BONDING – Good Chemistry – Montessori Muddle*
>
> *Posting by Lensyl Urbuno - A cute little video about ionic and covalent bonds by 10th grade chemistry student Eli Cirino) (1)*

General Remarks on Leadership

Leadership relationships and getting employees as well as teams connected are driven by finding the right people chemistry, along with the removal of silos throughout the business environment. Clear and well aligned goals across work groups can serve as building blocks that promote cross-functional connections and collaboration. Positive and inspiring interactions can even be the foundation for enhancing networks, for using different thinking perspectives, and for deepening the understanding of markets, as well as the customers, and even the industry as a whole. Finding common ground, similarities and comfort at all functional levels throughout the organization help serve as a way for leaders to focus the company strategies on the future. Connecting people fostered by open communication builds personal trust and authentic values.

Leadership relationships need to be flexible so that leaders are able to address business and organizational complexities along with newly surfacing challenges. A successful leader must have tremendous self-awareness to support their learning and growth of new managerial approaches, and to define creative actions that can lead to progressive outcomes. Strong problem-solving and decision-making on complex issues will impact the flow of information within teams and groups, resulting, hopefully, in positive achievements.

Building dynamic leadership relationships can follow a defined process. And, the investment of energy, time, and collaboration clearly supports the value of connections, especially since it drives constructive personal growth.

There are four components for building business relationships.

1. The Who – the framework for a true people-focus and realistic purpose

2. The Why – the definition and description of the specific targets and goals

3. The How – the collection of "data" and the diagnosis of assumptions

4. The What – the implementation of actions and assessment of results

Leaders are always working with others and collaborating to build value-oriented relationships so that they can strategically focus on addressing business challenges and needs. Leaders may not always have the answers or even have the specific required skills. Yet, as part of their leadership learning journey, they are continuously developing and growing new competencies and abilities. In so doing, they can make critical decisions and implement actions that are creatively coordinated so that teams can achieve their defined objectives and business direction.

Leadership and Internal Business Relationships

Leaders foster strong internal business relationships as well as partnerships, encouraging proactive connections between managers and employees. They build creative teams and collaborative work groups though trust that is focused on human behaviors. These relationships are based on many leadership competencies, including soft skill components such as compassion and integrity. Relationship-driven leaders practice and utilize key critical success factors to enhance their effectiveness and efficiencies along with their desired outcomes. As with all leadership activities, authenticity and realism can drive organizational growth as well as business changes, especially since they are established by people commitments and employee connections, as well as enhanced by leader presence and *human chemistry*.

> Simply put, the achievement of the company purpose and vision is based on the ability of the leader to provide several connecting components.

- Clear organizational direction for the future
- Simplicity of objectives based on defined boundaries
- Inspiring connections and partnerships
- Energizing and engaging relationships
- Authenticity in leadership behaviors
- Compassion with dedication and openness

So, what are the critical factors that drive connecting relationships and strategic business successes? There are nine primary complementary and interrelated leadership-relationship factors. They are pictorially represented below, followed by insightful details and quotations.

The Dynamic Relationship Wheel

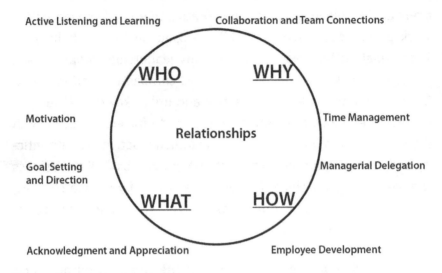

Effective Communications

Active Listening and Learning

Collaboration and Team Connections

WHO

WHY

Motivation

Relationships

Time Management

Goal Setting
and Direction

Managerial Delegation

WHAT

HOW

Acknowledgment and Appreciation

Employee Development

Effective Communications - Leaders need to move away from just talking that utilizes tell-assertive communication approaches. They need to learn to balance discussions and personal connections with a greater focus on active listening. Effectiveness of communications comes from true listening and the asking of logical as well as engaging questions. A key success component is having actual face-to-face conversations that are focused and uninterrupted. Ideas, thoughts, insights, and personal challenges need to be shared openly and successfully. This is rarely achieved via emails or tweets.

As per Oscar Wilde, *"Ultimately the bond of all companionships, whether in marriage or in friendship is conversation."* (2)

Oscar Wilde was an Irish poet and playwright during the 1880's and 1890's.

Every leader has their own style of communication. It may vary based on the specific situation or the immediate challenges that the individual is involved with at the time. Yet, each person will have a dominant style and area of comfort. Some individuals may be more assertive and tell-oriented, whereas others may be less assertive and more ask-oriented. Some individuals may be more focused on tasks and facts versus others who are more people focused and extroverted in nature. Regardless, in the business world, leaders need to have effective and impactful conversations that can lead to higher levels of commitment to specific strategic actions along with enhanced shared accountability. Their communications, conversations, and interactive connections all must drive business performance as well as strengthen personal relationships. In so doing, people develop, and organizations grow.

> As per Sherry Turkle, in her book entitled **Reclaiming Conversation – The Power of Talk in a Digital Age**, "Fully present to one another, we learn to listen. It's where we develop the capacity for empathy. It's where we experience joy of being heard, of being understood. And conversation advances self-reflection, the conversations with ourselves that are the cornerstone of early development and continue throughout life." (Page 3) "Reclaiming conversation is a step toward reclaiming our most fundamental human values. (Page 7) (3)

Collaboration and Team Connections - Successful leaders are good at building employee collaboration and at energizing small teams as well as large groups. A defined framework for team structure along with a team culture helps create a relationship-management focus. And, effective functioning work-teams can have a long-term competitive advantage, specifically, the ability to influence key business activities and to achieve sustainable results.

Interestingly, innovative teams using creative thinking approaches can impact strategies by using personal perspectives and the sharing of collective ideas and information. Even disagreements and some levels of conflict can result in strong achievement of goals and related projects. The building of team relationships is truly based on being strategic in nature and in driving dynamic connections to common values as well as to a clear vision.

Team effectiveness and the ability to support the organization can be further examined by looking at the many different team models that have been developed over the last 40 years. *The GRPI Model* (4) was created in 1977 by Rubin, Plovnick, and Fry, and it has maintained its value and impact over many years. It has four basic components. The "G" of the model defines the goals of the team. Goals can be ambitious at times, yet must require complete commitment. Clarity of purpose and the definition of the desired results need to be fully agreed to by the group. Deadlines are carefully laid out along with the establishment of critical priorities. The "R" is for the definition of team member roles as well as the identification of responsibilities. As part of the role definition, a team leader or co-leaders may be selected. The "P" of the model identifies the processes to be followed throughout the workflow. It can also help with the decision-making activities along with the allocation of resources. Finally, the most important piece of the model is the "I", since it is for interpersonal relationships and the primary foundation for all team interactions. Trust, collaboration, and communication defines the potential for team success. Goals and roles are clear, processes are followed, and interpersonal relationships develop and grow. These engaging teams are built on high levels of diversity specific to competencies and knowledge, as well as many evolving soft skills. The team or group leader drives the relationships through their openness and transparency. Risks are encouraged, problems are solved, and successful decisions are made as well as executed. The team grows with credibility and value to the organization, along with personal team partnerships.

Strategic Time Management - Leaders need to manage and energize organized activities that evolve into business actions. Establishing clear time lines along with potential completion target dates further dramatizes the importance of the "P" of the *GRPI Model*, specific to processes and workflow. Time management is a critical leadership skill that translates plans into actions, decisions, communication, opportunities, meetings, and eventually, into business results.

> ➤ Decisions need to have well defined deadlines. Individuals need to be identified specific to their roles and accountability to the timelines. There needs to be periodic reviews and clear strategic delegation of the defined actions that support the decisions. The leader examines each step so that the desired results can be achieved. People performance and their contributions are driven by good decisions.

> ➤ Communication of information specific to the actions plans need to be shared and understood by all colleagues. This includes individuals at multiple levels – executives, peers and direct reports. The leader, once again, needs to drive the flow and must make sure that the details are well disseminated.

> ➤ Opportunities for personal and business growth are the key drivers of results. Leaders need to embrace changes in the marketplace and use innovative approaches to meet customer needs or close existing gaps. And to best meet the evolving needs of the business, leaders must have the right people doing the right things along with a focus on new technology.

➢ Meetings help drive the action plans as an effective component of time management. Preparation is always critical for a successful meeting. And the leader builds discipline into the meeting format that is appropriate for the desired outcomes and results. Following a productive session, good follow-up is also important. It pulls all of the pieces together and carefully lays-out assignments, accountability, and deadlines.

So: Actions -- Decisions -- Communication -- Opportunities -- Meetings = Strategic Time Management

Effective and efficient time management is enhanced by leadership relationships and done without micro-managing or macro-managing. Strategically prioritized business objectives with clear purpose serves as the foundation for the leader to establish a work environment with an ideal plan and future vision. Both personal and company transformations are driven and supported by time managed actions.

Managerial Delegation - The key to leadership success is to involve all team members in the gathering of the details as well as facts, and in the decision-making activities. Business challenges need to be assessed, questions need to be reviewed, and issues need to be brought to the table and discussed openly. The utilization of complex thought processes must to be encouraged. Creative thinking and the acceptance of odd insights can lead to outstanding discoveries and fantastic solutions. Leaders should delegate authority so that the decisions that are made are strong, valued-based, and can meet the corporate objectives and long-term vision.

Leaders today are very busy dealing with complex, knowledge-driven and cost-competitive work environments. Delegation becomes a craft that can actually impact relationships. It is critical in getting the job done and in building trust in the quality of the outcomes. Team capabilities and skills can be developed as part of the delegation process. And, a positive work culture can be grown through managerial delegation. Yet, all leaders need to remember that they must continue to be committed to addressing the everyday business challenges to be successful.

- They need to keep leading by example and having a commitment to the achievement of strong and strategic performance.
- They need to keep evaluating team performance frequently specific to knowledge and skills along with the required learning and development needs.
- They need to provide regular feedback and personal coaching to team members.
- They need to build morale and increase respect between all team players.
- They need to assess processes and the organizational structure for effectiveness and business efficiencies.
- They need to provide acknowledgement and rewards for successful contribution.

Leaders use *human chemistry* to focus on leading others and on their professional responsibilities. This can best be achieved through different forms of managerial delegation to the team members. Of course, leaders must always remain fully engaged and strategically involved in the critical business activities. Again, a quick reminder that this is also an opportunity to develop knowledge, experiences, and competencies of others in the organization as well as within themselves. The resulting outcome can be getting more done in less time and, also, enhancing the enjoyment of work. Regardless, leaders need to be disciplined and focused, specifically on having deep accountability for corporate direction and personal actions.

Employee Development - Leaders need to help all employees grow and develop during their work experiences and career journey. They need to recognize the importance of improving skills and knowledge of the work population, and that, in turn, it clearly can encourage the enhancement of relationships between employees. Sharing with each other, learning from others, taking reasonable risks based on newly acquired competencies, all can absolutely maximize professional growth and personal connections. Learning and development can become the foundation of the culture of an organization, especially through the support of the leader. Leaders can even become teachers and coaches, helping get employees engaged in high-performance learning. In so doing, skills and competencies are enhanced at all levels and in all jobs. Individuals can be moved into new positions so that "on-the-job" learning can occur. And this is furthered through the actual application of the new capabilities specific to different roles and challenging positions.

Learning and development is a process of providing a diversity of forms and avenues for general growth. As already stated, building stronger talent becomes the foundation for valuing an organization's people and their performance contributions. This development-focused culture evolves as the learning is integrated into specific management processes and activities. Personal growth can impact innovation, drive higher levels of customer satisfaction, and improve time-to-market with new products as well as services. Employees should take time and be encouraged to reflect on their learnings, enhancing a stronger focus on long-term thinking and on the ability to handle change. The success of learning and development is built on unlocking the mind, uncovering strengths, and building relationships.

Leader-relationship evolution can also focus on employee career aspirations and on supporting activities that provide skills for goal achievements. The identification of new challenges needs to be a part of the training opportunities. Finding ways to draw out capabilities and talent in others, helping to dissect problems and issues, and driving individuals to make personal discoveries with hidden solutions – all become the foundation for the development mindset and culture. The leader establishes an engaging chemistry that is anchored in an employee development-orientated and a growth-focused environment.

> As per the Gallup Organization, *"Individuals who feel that their own development is being encouraged, and who have had opportunities to learn and grow, tend to have stronger engagement and performance."* (5)

Acknowledgment and Appreciation - Leaders can build relationships by recognizing the values each employee brings to the work environment. Work contributions need to be appreciated and acknowledged, and through feedback, both positive as well as constructive, helps demonstrate the impact an individual can have on the organization. Reinforcing successful actions and contributions builds partnerships. This can be further enhanced by leaders showing that they fully understand and recognize the importance of the commitments made by direct reports, colleagues, and employees at all levels of the company. Desired behaviors need to be praised with a depth of realistic enthusiasm that supports organizational values and culture. Delivering truthful, heartfelt, profound, and generous appreciation and gratitude clearly can impact business accomplishments and successes. Having high levels of openness and empowerment that are inspirational in nature can encourage the willingness by others to try new things, take risks, and go the extra mile. So, leaders create cultures that are focused on trust and on the encouragement to work hard and to contribute from the heart.

As per Judith Umlas, International Institute for Learning, Inc., *"When employees are engaged, they are passionate and feel a deeper connection to their work. Grateful leaders achieve the bottom line and foster a value-driven workforce to build stronger professional relationships with customers, stakeholders, and employees."* (6)

Relationships are built on communicating the importance of gratitude and through the art of demonstrating appreciation in the workplace environment. Both productivity and return on investment (ROI) can be increased through strong employee engagement and the fostering of employee recognition. This is accomplished by formal as well as informal approaches and programs. Always take the time as a leader to show thanks for excellent and outstanding contributions, and share the value openly. This is truly motivating for all individuals, specific to employees as internal customers and for product-users as external customers. Both require appreciation to enhance dedicated and engaging relationships, which in-turn can drive business successes.

Goal Setting and Direction - Leaders need to provide clear and motivating goals along with a specific focus on potential contributions to the company direction. They can help drive the value of each position and an employee's desire to have an effective impact on the business outcomes. Building progressive steps and delivering results becomes dependent on strong and connected employees that have jobs that are meaningful.

Leaders need to articulate the direction for the organization based on short-term objectives and long-term goals. They must translate the corporate vision into actions that may add to the bottom-line. There are many models associated with goal setting such as a "leadership bicycle analogy". (7) It was created during the 1990s by Lance Secretan, an author and public speaker. The front wheel of the bicycle provides the <u>direction</u> and the rear wheel provides the <u>power</u>. Secretan defines the back or rear wheel as the source of personal and organizational power – *"life-skill values based on accelerators – learning (knowledge and wisdom); empathizing (thoughts, feelings, and perspective); and listening (hearing and understanding)."* Besides power, an organization needs clear direction as per the bicycle's front wheel. Key is to balance the rear and front wheels to achieve the desired goal outcomes.

There is also a well-known goal model based on the word **SMART**. This is a mnemonic acronym associated with Peter Drucker's management objective concept. (8) The "S" is for specific. Goals need to be measurable, clear and not ambiguous. They should be motivating, the "M". A compelling goal needs to work for the individual, the leader, and the organization. And, as a motivating goal, it needs to be growth oriented for all three goal owners. Goals can have some level of stretch and challenge, yet they need to be attainable, the "A". And the "R". It is for relevant or realistic within the expectations of the organizational objectives. Finally, the "T" is specific to the trackability and time element of a goal. Basically, it defines the deadlines expected. This model for goal setting is based on these five specific components.

Leaders establish goals to support the vision and to enhance the focus on the desired end-points. They define milestones and ways of measuring achievements. As already stated, goals need to be motivating and can serve as a basis for personal growth and development, as well as providing some feeling of reward for key accomplishments. Leaders need to be careful to balance "power and direction", help maintain overall stability, and not get overly obsessive about goals.

As per Marshall Goldsmith, in his book **What Got You Here Won't Get You There – How successful people become even more successful**, *"Lasting goal achievement requires lots of time, hard work, personal sacrifice, ongoing effort, and dedication to a process that is maintained over years. And even if you pull that off, the rewards may not be all that you expect."* (9)

Motivation - Leaders motivate and inspire teams and employee groups through the clarity of purpose and an effective vision for the future. Each team member needs to feel fully empowered to make and implement good decisions. They need to feel that they are valued-adders to the overall organizational growth as well as the bottom-line team growth. Simply put, leaders can impact attitudes and behaviors that can actually influence abilities and competencies to contribute. Leaders are the drives of people and company performance, even during challenging times and demanding business environments. Increasing employee motivation can be accomplished by many actions, such as building confidence through the recognition of outstanding successes. Celebrating these contributions and also providing additional encouragement can result in getting employees to jump obstacles and resolve demotivating issues. Individuals become motivated to change their behaviors and even take steps outside of their comfort zones, and, surprisingly, find ways <u>not</u> to be overly consumed by business priorities.

Leaders can unlock energy and enthusiasm in employees. They use both extrinsic and intrinsic motivators, specifically low level or short-term motivators, and high impact or long-term motivators. Rewards and punishments, well known as the "carrot and stick" approach is short lived in the value of motivating. Moving to a focus on the desires to learn, develop and grow, and on building a better work environment can have stronger as well as longer lasting impact.

- Work needs to be fulfilling, fun, and enjoyable.
- It need to have purpose and meaning.
- Employees need to feel that they are growing and developing.
- Employees need to feel that they are contributors and that they are making a difference for the organization.
- There is less focus on compensation.
- Work needs to be stimulating and built on the utilization of individual strengths.
- It needs to be interesting and challenging.
- Employees need to feel empowered to bring about change by being self-directed and autonomous.
- They need to feel that they are elevating the organization as well as their own personal lives.

Motivation comes from the leader that shows appreciation and acknowledges successful contributions. Leaders are the drivers of commitment through the encouragement of risk-taking. They need to be willing to expose their passion for the company and the work-force, always actively engaging everyone from their head and from their heart.

Active Listening and Learning - True active listening by a leader represents full engagement with another individual. The leader removes distractions and does not jump to conclusions about intentions or meaning. They must try not to let interruptions enter into the conversations. High levels of self-awareness by the leader helps establish sincerity as well as demonstrate real interest in the discussion.

Active listening is a special skill and even an art. It is also a process and a craft of removing filters so that deep understanding and awareness can be established. This is a leadership competency based on seeking insights into important issues without just mentally preparing a reply. It is based on developing complete context and being fully present. It involves the mind as well as the body. The mind needs to be open, looking for the central theme, and analyzing what is being said by an individual along with what is not being said. The body requires eye contact, watching for nonverbal signs, and taking a position of not interrupting.

So, the listening and learning leader works with an open mind and engages by establishing presence. They must be full of energy and enthusiasm, and be truly alive as they focus on the sensitive needs of others. There are two clear steps that an active-listening leader can follow.

1. They need to look for patterns by listening carefully for specifics. They need to go beyond their own personal experiences, and attempt to understand an individual's beliefs, values, and attitudes. They learn about feelings, emotions and moods, finding strengths and opportunities to build on going forward.

2. They need to work to develop context based on what is being said. They must remove all judgement and use care not to over analyze or evaluate the current situation.

An active listener builds trust as a leader, enhancing their self-awareness and ability to influence. They build authentic context by listening and by having emotional intelligence.

As per Marshall Goldsmith (author or co-author of 32 books), "Listening is complete and sincere absorption. The mission of listening is to be so tuned into the other person's message that understanding becomes a copy-and-paste function from one mind to another." (10)

A short story on Listening

The following story supports the importance of listening, building trust and credibility, and a way of showing concern and understanding of others. This article was written by Gene Weingarten that appeared in The Washington Post during April 2007. It won a Pulitzer Prize based on the article's originality about an experiment – **_Violinist Joshua Bell played incognito in a Washington subway._** (11)

> *A man sat at a metro station in Washington DC and started to play the violin; it was a cold January morning. He played six Bach pieces for about 45 minutes. During that time, since it was rush hour, it was calculated that thousands of people went through the station, most of them on their way to work. Three minutes went by and a middle-aged man noticed there was a musician playing. He slowed his pace and stopped for a few seconds and then hurried up to meet his schedule. A minute later, the violinist received his first dollar tip: a woman threw the money in the till and without stopping continued to walk. A few minutes later, someone leaned against the wall to listen to him, but the man looked at his watch and started to walk again. Clearly, he was late for work.*
>
> *The one who paid the most attention was a 3-year-old boy. His mother tugged him along, hurried but the kid stopped to look at the violinist. Finally, the mother pushed hard, and the child continued to walk turning his head all the time. This action was repeated by several other children. All the parents without exception, forced them to move on. In the 45 minutes the musician played, only 6 people stopped and stayed for a while. About 20 gave him money but continued to walk their normal pace. He collected $32. When he finished playing and*

silence took over, no one noticed it. No one applauded, nor was there any recognition.

No one knew this, but the violinist was Joshua Bell, one of the best musicians in the world. He played one of the most intricate pieces ever written with a violin worth 3.5 million dollars. Two days before his playing in the subway, Joshua Bell sold out at a theater in Boston and the seats averaged $100.

This is a real story. Joshua Bell playing incognito in the metro station was organized by the Washington Post as part of a social experiment about perception, taste and priorities of people. The outlines were: in a commonplace environment at an inappropriate hour: Do we perceive beauty? Do we stop to appreciate it? Do we recognize the talent in an unexpected context? One of the possible conclusions from this experience could be: If we do not have a moment to stop and listen to one of the best musicians in the world playing the best music ever written, how many other things are we missing?

Leadership and Building Relationships with an Established Team

Joining an existing team as the new leader requires a clear approach and process specific to building a dynamic and effective partnership. The leader needs to communicate and connect with the group from the heart and with total authentic openness. All activities must focus on interactions that enhance presence and establish trust. There is a need to align the team goals and actions with the long-term organizational strategies as well as vision. Team members need to be made to feel valued for their past contributions and empowered to make key impactful inputs for future business results. The new leader of this existing team must have personal self-awareness of their own competencies and abilities to drive group performance.

There are four building blocks that can be followed to drive a potentially successful team partnership by a new leader.

Phase One – **Listen & Learn**

Understanding the team roles, responsibilities, strengths, and challenges.

The team leader needs to actively listen to all team members. By not making any initial changes or creating a pre-conceived plan, the leader can build confidence and reassurance with the group and demonstrate a commitment to their participation. A great learning environment is encouraged with the leader, getting to understand team strengths and talent, specific challenges, and their needs and desires, especially with an ability to enhance personal growth. The leader needs to gain a full understanding of the roles, responsibilities, goals, and group approaches of the team members. This is accomplished through active listening.

The new leader becomes, as per the Wilson Learning Social Styles Model that was referenced in Chapter Four, more analytical and amiable in their communication approach. An *amiable leader* functions and connects with the group individuals by being more ask-assertive and more people-directed responsive. Being a more *analytical leader*, they gain insights by being more task oriented, building on the facts, data, and the numbers. Care must be taken that they are not perceived as cold and overly structured based on the use of logic in the gathering of information. The new leader needs to be flexible and versatile in their approaches to connecting and engaging with the team. It takes energy, commitment, and enthusiasm to be effective and value-oriented. Spoken words and nonverbal messages need to be focused and clear. The communication can contain aspects of attitude, personal values, and moods. And, the leader needs to build their presence by virtually sharing values, priorities, and methodologies that have impacted past business outcomes.

Phase Two – **Plan & Strategize**

Building on current team goals, purpose, processes, and approaches.

The team leader helps the group move to a planning stage and to reinforce a positive approach to driving tasks and objectives of the team. These connections and communications are built on the empowerment to make decisions based on established processes of problem-solving. Together the leader and the team members analyze, conduct modeling and root cause evaluations, and address strategies for potential solutions or changes. Together, they enhance the way logic is applied along with personal thoughts and information reasoning. The new leader respects existing team approaches to challenges, and the leader and team members can actually grow together.

The leader must take time to understand the various barriers facing the team and tackle roadblocks together that will be found on the path to the best solutions. Using past or conventional techniques may not be adequate or optimal, and new approaches may have to be applied. Imposing too many limitations can cause a narrow focus, just as over using aspects of common sense that can result in under thinking a possible solution. The leader and the team members must balance their intellectual reasoning from their "head" with their passion, feelings, and emotions from their "heart". The group and the leader turn decisions and solutions into well designed and clear actions. Just as with problem-solving, the decision process follows specific steps – define / diagnose / analyze / act / test. As mentioned in Chapter Three, the strategic approaches and plans are a result of balancing several components – fast versus slow; risk versus reward; advantages versus disadvantages; complexity versus simplification; instinct versus logic; thoughts versus emotions. Together, with collective intelligence of the group members and the leader, they can demonstrate confidence and good judgment with solid decisions and plans.

Phase Three – **Act & Implement**

Driving team creativity, risk taking, and group thinking.

The team partnership is well on its way. Roles and responsibilities are clear and team members are growing in their relationships with each other. There is a strong focus on long-term organizational strategies. Challenges are being addressed and hurdles are being jumped together. Implementing decisions and taking actions are done with high levels of creativity and engagement. The leader is moving out of their comfort zone and taking risks with the support of the team. They have the courage to take actions without the fear of failing. The team, as well as the leader, can grow successfully in their evolving roles.

The greatest challenge in the implementation of actions by both the new leader and the team is to have courage in making bold decisions and being innovative with nontraditional ideas. Risk-taking requires skills of utilizing past experiences, details, and in-depth knowledge of the team situations. All risks differ in size and requirements, with all actions impacting financial investments and business outcomes. The group as a team rises above fear and human emotions to gain the competitive advantage.

Phase Four – **Review & Evaluate**

Assessing team decisions, successes, and growing relationships.

The leader needs to continuously evaluate team performance and also accept feedback from the group members. The team makes changes and upgrades objectives based on the evolving business needs. The leader has built trust and gained the confidence of the team. The new leader is no longer new, and they have been able to foster engagement, collaboration, and job satisfaction. True partnerships have been formed and the leader as well as the team individuals are able to make more risky decisions successfully with courage. Everyone continues to grow with energy and build new strengths, competencies, and skills.

This fourth phase is built on team relationships. The existing team connections throughout the four phases are based on the right chemistry and finding ways to remove silos from all business activities. Common ground, similarities, and comfort with a new leader will help serve as a way to enhance strategies for the future, and as a way of connecting the team members with each other based on consistent values. Going forward under the new leader, the team's effectiveness needs to become a sustainable competitive advantage.

As per Patrick Lencioni, author of several team-related books, teams need to focus on five areas:

1. Trust – the willingness to be vulnerable and open, and to build on strengths.

2. Engaging – the ability to disagree and challenge to find the best solutions.

3. Commitment – putting new ideas on the table and buy into genuine decision-making.

4. Accountability – adhering to decisions.

5. Results – having clear focus.

In Patrick's book – **Overcoming The Five Dysfunctions of a Team**, (12) he builds a model based on overcoming the five dysfunctions:

1. *Absence of Trust*

2. *Fear of Conflict*

3. *Lack of Commitment*

4. *Avoidance of Accountability*

5. *Inattention to Results*

It is also interesting to connect the four-phase approach – the four building blocks - to the learning and development process used by the IDD Leadership Group. The existing team members and the new leader are always on a continuous growth and learning journey.

Step One – Assess & Understand

Conducting a focused assessment and identification of the needs specifically required to bring about individual as well as organizational change and growth.

Step Two – Plan & Design

Establishing a clear purpose and plan based on realistic as well as achievable goals along with desired outcomes.

Step Three – Develop & Deliver

Implementing action-oriented learning events and engaging workshops that can drive change, growth, and valued results.

Step Four – Evaluate & Discover

Reviewing and evaluating the success of all program activities and the impact on an evolving organization over time.

Under the direction and support of the new leader, the existing team can grow together, jump challenging hurdles, and impact long-term organizational goals. Utilizing the four building blocks can take weeks and months, and can result in the enhancement of team member engagement as well as relationships for years. As the new leader has evolved with the existing team, the individuals making up the team have always been the critical focus for the leader. Basically, the key has been to know the people and to fully understand their personal needs and drivers. Collaborating regularly, noticing contributions with real passion, and taking time to celebrate successes together have been the extended drivers.

- The leader needs to <u>inspire</u> the team, unlock their minds, motivate creativity and curiosity, and grow innovative behaviors.
- The leader needs to <u>drive</u> to uncover the strengths of the team, build engagement and relationships, and energize the desire to address challenges.
- The leader needs to help <u>deliver</u> the strategic power to the team, develop a learning culture, and build business results.

Leadership and External Business Relationships

Leaders also need to foster external relationships and constantly enhance connections outside of the organization. They use many of the competencies already described, such as effective communications, team connections, time management, appreciation, and active listening. Deepening the customer connections is primarily based on two primary factors – focused relationships and external collaboration.

Factor One - Customer Focused Relationships

Leaders need to drive a focus on customers, to fully understand their needs, and to leverage business activities to meet their desired expectations. Team and group decisions are based on the facts and insights into customer requirements specific to the needed support as well as potential areas for desired improvements. Also critical is to fully understand the customer markets and aspects of key success-drivers of a business.

By learning and gaining insights regarding the details about future customers and potential marketplace needs, a leader must enhance their relationships through many contacts. There are several factors that can impact these partnerships that will build long-term value for both organizations.

Discovery of wants and needs

Looking to meet and connect with customers and fully understand their specific needs and wants. Critical for success is to gain insight and understanding into the hurdles and challenges that customers have and the problems that need immediate attention and to be solved. The commitment to growing external knowledge and customer requirements truly can enhance business relationships.

Market connections and instincts

Finding trends in the established market environments can help establish direction for personal relationships and partnerships. Going after the right things will be based on innovative approaches to creating new products and services. And, gaining a full handle on competitive activities can also have a significant impact on future business connections.

Brand identity

Establishing a clearly developed-brand name along with a brand-look can help build trust and value into a company and its products. And connecting this value of the brand with innovative approaches to products and markets can be enhanced through supportive behaviors that are focused on current and future customer relationships.

Building loyalty

Leaders need to help employees connect and foster relationships that are focused on customer satisfaction via the right price structure, and of course, top-level quality. Exceeding expectations of the customer means doing it right and providing the desired products as well as services. And, loyalty can be further enhanced through effective business friendships and a willingness to be open by sharing insights on a personal level.

Factor Two - External collaboration and synergy with the customer

Building alignment of organizational priorities, team goals, and customer needs and wants can be driven by relationships. Collaboration with customers and sharing of ideas along with different viewpoints demonstrates the willingness to listen and to discover their specific needs. A collaborative mindset enhances creative interactions and true partnerships. It helps new ideas and concepts come to the surface and to be shared with openness and flexibility. General conversations and the exchange of information can increase innovation and product development. Some ideas can be based on successful discoveries as well as disappointing failures.

The overall outcome may be the accelerated launches of new products and new services.

<u>Closing insights specific to external business relationships</u>

Again, it goes back to leadership that is based on achieving maximum contributions through cooperative employee as well as customer relationships. Leaders need to create and facilitate collaborative and transparent processes as well as open communication. Group decision-making must be based on input from everyone, even though at times there may be conflict and resistance. Yet, these collaborative customer-based teams need strong ownership and commitment to the desired actions. Leaders enhance their trust and respect as they listen more to ideas from others, and are truly appreciated as collaborative relationship-builders.

Leaders Building Dynamic Relationship

Leaders connecting with employees, teams, and customers

Personal Story - #1

Even though I started my business career as a technical coordinator for a small family-owned engineering firm, it was the position as product manager at Essex Chemical Corporation that launched my business leadership learning experiences and journey. The key to my successes and rewards was the building of both internal and external authentic and rewarding relationships.

In the early 1980s, I was employed by Essex in New Jersey, a developer and manufacturer of a diverse portfolio of chemical products. As with every organization that I joined throughout my career, the business was eventually acquired by a much larger company. In this case, the new organization was Dow Chemical with its headquarters in Midland, Michigan. They sold off specific components of Essex and they quickly assimilated into the Dow world the products and the materials manufactured by Essex Specialty Products.

Hired as a product manager, I was responsible for a product call *Betabrace*. (13) This material was a reinforcing composite that was used in the automotive industry to reinforce the outer skin of a car – the body sheet steel. By the middle of the 1980s, the outer body skin was being down gaged to reduce the weight of an automobile so that gas mileage could be improved. *Betabrace* was a dye cut "patch" made of carefully formulated epoxy and woven fiberglass material. The patch had the ability to adhere to oily sheet steel and cure during the paint prep baking processes. It was placed on the inner surface of the out-body panel to reinforce areas that potentially could be damaged by the vehicle owner – such as door "hipping" – a dent into the door, and deck lid "palm printing" – a dent in the trunk lid on closure.

As the product "owner" and marketing leader for *Betabrace*, my overall goal and general mission was to increase the usage of the reinforcing material by all of the car manufactures on a global basis. The primary focus was with Ford, General Motors, and Chrysler. Building and maintaining connections and relationships was very important. A quick personal discovery identified the critical nature of these true connections. It was the relationship leadership skills that became the foundation for success. And several philosophical factors needed to be implemented – both <u>internally</u> to Essex/Dow, and <u>externally</u> with the automobile manufacturers. They were:

- To enhance interpersonal engagements based on truly taking the time to get to know the organizational cultures as well as the primary individuals involved in the *Betabrace* development, sales, and end-user approvals.
- To actively listen to all product "drivers" within Dow Chemical (Essex Specialty Products) and the car companies, and to have many constructive conversations of significance.
- To learn to focus on all of the needs and desires of the customers as well as to become deeply involved with employees throughout the company, and to be a less self-centered product manager.
- To build trust in all of the relationships, internal and external, demonstrating a genuine interest in people by dedicating time and effort to others.
- To have regular live contact and face-to-face meetings, always working on building and growing strong, long-lasting, and engaging "personal partnerships".

So, here is a "picture" of how my product management skills and knowledge developed, and how the *Betabrace* product revenue dramatically grew in three years. Both components were a fast evolution. And the focus was always on three pieces – my colleagues, the customers, and the product itself.

Well, a formulated product starts with a dedicated and committed chemistry / R&D team. The product had already been created and approved by several automotive engineering groups. This specific product line had achieved approximately a half-million dollars in sales early on in its introduction. It was still being further reviewed by customers for additional application needs as well as for the very specific product requirements. So, there was the arrival of a new product manager (me) that was very focused on being supportive of all needs and highly engaged in developing strong relationships. Appreciation and interest in product value became a positive component and driving force for success. Some formula adjustments were made, changes to the manufacturing process were implemented, and redesigns were embraced so that the desired products and configurations were produced. By the close of my first year as product manager, sales revenue results came in around four million dollars. Aggressive relationships with the sales organization and with customers clearly helped drive this fantastic accomplishment.

A dynamic *Betabrace* team with representation by manufacturing, R&D, sales, finance, and senior management helped enhance the continued use of the product by the automotive companies. Product tweaks were made when necessary. Full support of the marketing group also drove sales revenue. Brand recognition was a special piece of the success specific to the focus on the product name, logo, and packaging. The product became a highly recognized material that could support the needs to build a better, fuel efficient automobile. As product manager, I made my presence known within the assembly facilities, demonstrating the commitment of the company to the customers' needs and desires, always helping to bring the expected value of the partnership.

The product sales revenue grew each year to about 8 million in the second year and 12 million in the third year. Connecting and building relationships with automotive manufacturing engineers, management, and even the line-production workers, all had a major impact. I was not recognized by my name within the auto plants, but rather, as *Mr. Betabrace.* Following a specific approach, "just-in-time" products were close to the production utilization areas. And *Betabrace* materials was not in a plain craft box. No, not *Betabrace*! It was in a white, high-end box with a distinctive black and red logo.

Relationships at many levels, the product value, product name recognition, and engaging communications both internal to Dow/Essex and the automotive manufacturing sites, all became the critical *human chemistry* for the outstanding growth and product success. The *Betabrace* Team was a true and dedicated group with everyone worked well together. Even though there were occasional disagreements, the team always found ways to tackle challenges. There were regular group meetings at all sites – R&D in New Jersey, manufacturing in Michigan, and sales around the world. These team players would go above and beyond to accomplish expectations driven by the product manager. Personal time and dinners were common. I made it a point to be in the lab, and in the product manufacturing plant, and in sales and marketing meeting, and in the automotive manufacturing facilities. Outstanding achievements were a result of true relationships, open communication, dynamic collaboration, and personal commitment. These were authentically realistic partnerships. What a great story to share. Thanks!

Personal Story - #2

This is a personal relationship and team story that is based on some interesting and inspirational discoveries. It is about connecting with personal insights that are associated with engagement, compassion, and collaboration. Building presence and experiencing face-to-face activities clearly can enhance trust, optimism, and a transparent, straight-forward reality with people. This more recent experience in my business world was during employment with the Getinge Group in Sweden. As part of a three-day human resource strategy planning meeting north of Stockholm, there were many interactive discussions and presentations by a group of nine executives. Four of the individuals were top global leaders, and the other five of us were carefully selected team support members holding various VP or director roles. The evening of the first day of this engaging meeting resulted in a very special event. It was the Fall of 2010.

The diversity of the group was a very important success factor. There were three levels of leadership – one senior corporate leader, three divisional business leaders, and five human resource leaders from different roles and business areas. We were all well connected prior to this gathering, even though we brought many various backgrounds and competencies to the table. This diverse group of leaders had several great components – different ages, three women, and we represented five different global geographical areas – Sweden, Denmark, Germany, UK and the US. All of us had a variety of past business experiences as well as varying lengths of time in leadership positions.

So, the night went as follows. We all walked in the dark with candles for a good half hour through the woods to a small cabin. This little place was built in the early 1800s, and it had only two rooms, one for our coats, and the other equipped with a very large table, surrounded by chairs. The table was beautifully decorated with cheeses, fruit, breads, and wonderful wine as well as beer. We sat around the cozy table, sharing stories of all sorts, jokes, and challenging experiences. What was occurring throughout the evening was the formation of memorable connections and long-term relationships based on openness and personal vulnerability. The human side of life both in the business world as well as in our personal lives grew and established a never-ending belief in each other as business partners and as friends. Enhancement of relationships was clearly achieved. We discovered that we are just people, always facing regular challenges as well as successes in life, and that we are just individuals growing throughout our life's journey. Memories were made. Respect and appreciation was grown. Further understanding into our special leadership competencies was built on our evolving relationships. Once again, it was about our *human chemistry* and our leadership learning journey.

General Summary on Leadership and the Importance of Relationships

Leadership is based on the abilities and skills to build awareness of the behaviors of colleagues and to influence others along with providing positive motivation. Leaders need to continuously build and establish their credibility and trust in all internal and external relationships. Effective emphasis must be on engaging interactions and outstanding communications with team members. This will foster strong business results and outcomes. Leaders need to be transparent, emotionally intelligent, and use supportive behaviors with others. They must be genuine and authentic in demonstrating appreciation of all connections and partnerships.

Leadership is about being fully involved and present with people beyond just setting goals and strategies. As already stated several times, key is to develop and grow successful and meaningful relationships. Leaders must have personal self-awareness, an ability to motivate individuals and team members, to find inner empathy, and to have a willingness to enhance their social skills. Yes, leadership is complex. One must use all components of the mind, heart and body. As detailed in Chapter Four, emotional intelligence has given a clear picture that leadership is extremely challenging, and that self-awareness is a critical component. Managing and growing relationships effectively is the foundation for building trust and successes.

Great leadership is built on great relationships and *human chemistry*!

In the closing of this chapter, I want to share another fun yet informative story. Relationships are based on many components, such as the ability to employ exceptional observing and actively listening skills. Finding what is on the minds of others, and the sharing of insights and wisdom without any judgement or criticism, can help build actions with presence.

This story is from <u>Character Quality Stories</u> entitled ***Woman at Airport Waiting Area eats another Man's Cookies by Mistake.*** (14)

A young lady was waiting for her flight in the boarding room of a big airport. As she would need to wait many hours, she decided to buy a book to spend her time. She also bought a package of cookies. She sat down in an armchair, in the VIP room of the airport, to rest and read in peace. Beside the armchair where she had placed the packet of cookies, a man sat down in the next seat, opened his magazine and started reading. When she took out the first cookie, the man took one also. She just thought: *"What a nerve! If I was in the mood I would punch him for daring!"* For each cookie she took, the man took one too. This was infuriating her, but she didn't want to cause a scene. When only one cookie remained, she thought: *"oh...What would this abusive man do now?"* The, the man, taking the last cookie, divided it into half, giving her one half. Ah! That was too much! She was much too angry now! In a huff, she took her book, her things and stormed to the boarding area. When she sat down in her seat, inside the plane, she looked into her purse to get her eyeglasses. To her surprise, her packet of cookies was there, untouched, unopened! She felt so ashamed! She realized that she was wrong.......She had forgotten that her cookies were put into her purse. The man had divided his cookies with her, without feeling angered or bitter. ....while she had been very angry, thinking that she was dividing her cookies with him. And now there was no chance to explain herself... nor to apologize.

Remember, even with strong relationships and personal connections, there are four things that you cannot recover:

> The stone...after it is thrown!
> The word...after it has been said!
> The occasion...after it is lost!
> The time...after it is gone!

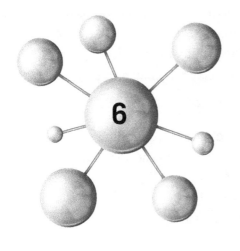

LEADERSHIP AND COMMUNICATIONS FROM THE HEAD AND THE HEART

Leaders as great connectors, conversationalists, and relationship builders.

The Chemistry Connection

There are 118 elements on the Periodic Table of Elements and the chart is structured based on atomic numbers and electron configurations. The elements are grouped into specific locations as per chemical properties. The Table was first published in 1869 and not all of the elements had been discovered. What is amazing is that these 118 elements can chemically combine and react into thousands and thousands of various structures and materials.

Sodium is a chemical element with the symbol Na and atomic number 11. It is an alkali metal that is soft, silvery-white, and a highly reactive metal. It was discovered in 1807. Sodium is the sixth most abundant element in the Earth's crust. Chlorine is a chemical element with the symbol Cl and atomic number 17. It is not found as an element in nature, only as a compound. Chlorine is a yellow-green gas at room temperature, discovered in 1774. These two elements can bond into an inorganic compound that is well known, NaCl, salt.

Communicating, clarifying and describing chemical structures can be confusing, especially with eleven elements that have symbols derived from their Latin names, such as sodium (Na) or Natrium. Another example is gold, Au, from the Latin word Aurum.

((As per a shirt that is worn by my grandson – there is a picture of the Periodic Table of Elements printed on the shirt with a statement at the bottom – "I wear this shirt periodically".))

The reality is that confusions can be removed from communications once the details are carefully shared and explained. Leaders need to be great connectors and communicators, always authentically focused on others and on delivering messages that are value-oriented. Effective communicating leaders propel organizations to produce incredible and successful results. This competency of delivering information and details on business direction based on clarity and inspiration can help drive innovative ideas into new possibilities. It also supports the abilities for the employee population to meet progressive goals as well as to achieve an outstanding vision.

General Remarks on Leadership

Leadership is an art, a science, and a craft in the connection with people. It is based on *human chemistry*. As carefully detailed in Chapters Four and Five, leaders can influence how people think and behave. They can impact individuals as well as organizational cultures by being creative in their approaches and inspiring in their messages. They can enhance meaningful internal colleague relationships as well as external customer partnerships. Authentic leadership through effective communication can build people connections so that the established objectives and desired goals can be driven to successful levels and stimulate progressive organizational growth.

As per Peter Schwartz, author of **The Art of the Long View**, - clearly states that *"Designing strategic conversations leads to continuous organizational learning about key decisions and priorities. Yet, the most successful leaders are those who will see their fundamental work not as making-decisions, but as making mutual understanding."* (1)

Leaders as Great Communicators, Connectors, and Conversationalists

Leaders need to show commitment and enthusiasm in their communications as well as in their negotiations. They need to drive truthful, open, and credible connections with the entire employee population based on factual accuracy and information details. There is more "asking and listening" than "telling". Leaders can clearly demonstrate self-confidence and empathy along with strong interpersonal and social skills to enhance their connections and *human chemistry*.

Great leadership communication is based on a real and authentic focus on people as well as on an understanding of their needs. The key is to be seen by others as using connections and conversations with consistency, and not flip-flopping of ideas or false promises. By demonstrating high levels of integrity in all relationships, trust can be enhanced, and the respect of the leader can be further reinforced. And, one must recognize that communication is a two-way process – the sending of a message and the receiving of a message. It is an exchange or flow of information, ideas, and even personal feelings. Critical for success is that the content of the transmitted message must be fully understandable, realistically rational, and have a very clear purpose. Leaders need to be fully aware that there are even nonverbal elements that need to be grasped. They are specific to eye contact, gestures and the body language of both the sender and the receiver.

Effective and impactful communication requires open channels. During conversations and the sharing of information, certain levels of flexibility need to exist based on current organizational situations and business challenges. Leaders are constantly and continuously building relationships, showing genuine interest in others, and providing extrinsic as well as intrinsic motivation. They are connecting with employees and encouraging transparency with their actual messages and with their audiences, the message receivers. Leadership involves coaching and counseling, coordinating plans, evaluating input, and providing supervisory insights. So, effective leaders are always communicating and sharing ideas, and are having conversations regarding company expectations, direction and goals.

On a simple level, there are three possible ways to improve and enhance leadership communications.

1. *Encourage feedback*

    Check how messages are being received by getting feedback and by evaluating how information was interpreted and understood. Requesting constructive and honest responses is a positive framework for building engagement and internal connections.

2. *Listen effectively*

> Provide an environment of support that encourages the ability to listen for creative ideas beyond the facts. Both the leader and the message receivers need to be open minded so that the total perspective to information can be gained. Active listening is done via physical and mental messaging.

3. *Reduce barriers and problems*

> Leaders need to make an effort to reduce misunderstanding of information. Words need to be clear and there must be an attempt to remove biases and defensiveness, as well as stress and ego. Perceptions and preconceived attitudes can be distracting and need to be properly managed.

Leadership communications need to be more like conversations so that they can help build relationships. When information is exchanged – slow it down, keep it simple, be open, listen actively, and show enthusiasm. Message clarity builds leader trust and respect along with employee engagement.

Now, a detailed examination of five key success factors that are foundational for leadership communication effectiveness.

One: Leader Communication with Interpersonal Self-Awareness

Leaders need high levels of self-awareness so that they can enhance their ability to clearly communicate company direction, and to drive consistency of organizational values, which in turn, can impact successful business outcomes. The creative and charismatic communication capabilities of leaders will help their connection with employees and indirectly support the personal learning and growth of others. And, leaders must never forget to utilize their own emotions and find ways to positively demonstrate empathy.

As already stated, communicating effectively is based on the messages being sent as well as on the messages being received, and on the successful interpretation of the words being shared. The statements and remarks can be powerful and influential, yet also simple and without judgement. There should be a congruency between the verbal and nonverbal message specific to its clarity of content and the confidence in the delivery. And, of course, trust is necessary for open and effective communication.

Through personal self-awareness of actual drivers as well as motivators, leaders are able to communicate thoughtfully with employees. They know how to frame their messages effectively without stereotyping or prejudicial biases so that they can influence the minds and behaviors of others along with impactful interactions. Being open and willing to self-disclose values, beliefs, and even attitudes can enhance their people connections. Clearly, this is based on interpersonal self-awareness by the leader, specific to "language" associated with the sharing and delivery of messages along with the general interactions. The ability to share information and ideas should occur without fear or anxiety associated with the transactional communications. Relationships can grow with unique and special connections, and be reinforced by different perspectives. As stated earlier, trust encourages a willingness to share thoughts, feelings and ideas based on self-confidence. Listening for understanding and having strong communications influence partnerships that will result in achieving the organizational long-term vision.

Two: Leader Communication with Active Listening and Observing

Communication is about speaking and sharing a message, and about listening and receiving a message. Both take energy, commitment, and enthusiasm to be effective and value-oriented. The spoken words and nonverbal messages need to be focused and clear. They can contain aspects of attitude, personal values, and moods. Yet, the message must always have purpose specific to providing information, sharing understanding, or supporting the solution to a problem.

Misunderstandings and confusion in communication can result in inaccurate interpretation of the meaning of the ideas, opinions or thoughts. Some messages can be overly complex in that they address too many issues and may contain too many details. This can result in an outcome that is incorrect based on preconceived conclusions as well as judgments. Communicating without a clear direction and focused purpose, results in contradictions and confusing facts or points.

Besides being a strong and well-composed communicator, a leader must also be an active listener. And in so doing, this approach will actually encourage the same methods and behaviors from others. The use of active listening demonstrates an understanding and interest in viewpoints and ideas from all sources. This approach to listening even utilizes feedback to verify agreement with the content and acknowledgment of the meaning. Communication and active listening will also take advantage of nonverbal facial connections along with eye contact to build psychological presence. And, there is always a need to carefully balance silence (saying nothing) with questioning (clarifying understanding).

> As per the Dalai Lama – *"When you talk, you are only repeating what you already know; but when you listen, you may learn something new".* (2)

The leader must also be an effective observer, gaining full context of various situations and encounters. These observing and listening leaders help mobilize employees throughout the organization to meet the challenges expected of them and to continuously build adaptive behaviors within the company population. Leaders may not have all the answers to situations as well as issues, and may not always be right. Yet, they need to know their people and understand the complexities and challenges that can drive performance. The observing leader develops the ability to feel the pulse of the organization and to be able to recognize employee patterns of functionality as well as dysfunctionality. Stepping back from the daily demands of decisions-making and action-implementation, a leader needs to carefully observe and reflect on the requirements of the company. In so doing, they can better drive the inspirational vision and make sure that it is fully aligned with the overall strategies. Active listening and engaging observing are both critical components of leadership communication.

> As per Albert Einstein – *"To raise new questions, new possibilities, to regard old problems from a new angle, requires creative imagination and marks real advances in science".* (3)

Three: Leader Communication with Engagement and Connections

Driving organizational results for immediate as well as long-term outcomes is about leaders that interact and connect with the workforce population. These behaviors by leaders help build a versatile culture which enhances productivity, improves employee retention, and drives business successes.

> Judith Umlas, author of **Grateful Leadership** and leader of the International Institute for Learning Inc. states *"When employees are engaged, they are passionate and feel a deeper connection to their work. Grateful leaders achieve the bottom line and foster a value-driven workforce to build stronger professional relationships with customers, stakeholders, and employees".* (4)

Employee engagement is associated with leadership connections and internal communications at a personal level. Meaningful relationships can be grown so that everyone is better informed regarding short-term objectives and the corporate long-term direction and vision. Leaders remove any form of ego and show a passion for employee involvement, specific to the products and services that can be provided, and for the impactful importance of commitment at the customer level.

Developing rapport, engagement, and connections are all based on several factors.

- Listening and caring for employees and their work environment is critical. This personal awareness promotes positive emotions with decision-making and problem-solving processes.
- Acknowledging successes both financial and non-financial achievements can have a dramatic impact on engagement. Recognition and appreciation are powerful behaviors that can go a long way, especially by celebrating, praising, and rewarding contributions.
- Accepting feedback regarding communications and the sharing of learned self-awareness can help promote involvement and reinforce connections.
- Collaborating enhances partnerships based on working and contributing toward a common purpose and company vision. Internal communication plans and policies will drive consistency in business activities and influence the organizational culture at the personal level.

Leaders need to engage and connect with the entire work population by demonstrating their commitment of being open, honest, and authentic in their communications. This will raise the leader's credibility, trust, and respect. Effective leaders go beyond just re-lationships. They are continuously building on their personal self-awareness by listening with depth of understanding and interest, as well as with emotion. To achieve the greatest company outcomes, the leader must always celebrate successes, recognize individual contributions openly, and praise workers with sincerity and enthu-siasm. It is about true and heartfelt gratitude and appreciation. This form of commitment will drive employee engagement and long-term connections.

Four: Leader Communication with a Learning and Development Focus

Effective leadership is built on outstanding people development and on the utilization of powerful learning programs with value-oriented content. Employees, as learners, need to have the correct skills, tools, and knowledge so that they can make strong contri-butions. These learners must be inspired and empowered to build their capabilities and to grow their desired performance competen-cies with new levels of awareness and thinking.

Leaders are always seeking out new development approaches and methodologies as well as gaining deeper understanding specific to learning needs and desires of others. They must support a learn-ing and development oriented culture based on informal learning, mobile technologies, competency development, mentoring and coaching, instructor-led training, and on-the-job growth activities. It is a balancing act of driving value specific to "classroom-based" (face-to-face interactive learning) and "virtually-driven" (on-line, self-driven) learning. And, experiential, personalized components should be blended into all approaches, such as stretch assignments and job shadowing.

Leaders need to communicate the importance of personal learn-ing and development that focuses on growing talent at all levels.

Learning is a life-long journey for employees and a beneficial investment for the organization. There must be a strong commitment in establishing a talent development mindset and culture, especially in a challenging "VUCA" world – one with an increase in volatility, uncertainty, complexity, and ambiguity. Employee skills and competency expectations are increasing and changing more rapidly. The workforce landscape of tomorrow will clearly require new and more diverse capabilities along with broader personal employee insights.

Building learning strategies can follow several steps. Assessments need to occur regularly regarding current employee experiences as well as future required skills to be strong contributors. Such assessments need to be conducted on an on-going basis. Learning expectations and outcomes need to be carefully define. Focused, prioritized, and relevant programs and activities need to be implemented. And, the learnings must be applied within an individual's job, along with specific follow-up plans. Ultimately, well executed learning and development components will result in the improvement of organizational performance and productivity.

Successful learning cultures that are evolving and growing are reinforced by face-to-face and engaging interactions as well as communications. Leaders need to promote collaboration and relationships throughout the organizations. As stated earlier, leaders need to actively listen, openly communicate, and realistically connect with employees.

> As per Sardek Love, president and founder of Infinity Consulting and Training Solutions, a global management and development consulting firm, - *"Talent development is so vast and wide, but when I start looking at what we've been doing traditionally. I think one of the greatest challenges*

that talent development has right now is equipping people and organizations to continuously grow". (5)

Five: Leader Communication with Inspiration and Encouragement

Leaders need to inspire people and to create an organizational culture based on creativity, commitment, and engagement. The focus of the leader is exemplified by an authentic passion and enthusiasm for excellence. Inspirational leadership must come from both the head and the heart. Leaders are always inspiring the workforce with a strong connection to creative thinking and value-driven relationships. These leaders have high levels of self-awareness and a willingness to openly self-disclose personal insights as well as business challenges in a caring and down-to-earth way.

> Joseph Jaworski, author of **Synchronicity: The Inner Path of Leadership**, states that "*Leadership is all about the release of human possibilities...the capacity to inspire the* people in the group...to help them get centered and operate at peak capacity. A key element of this capacity is communicating to people that you believe they matter, that you know they have something important to give. The confidence you have in others will to some degree determine the confidence they have in themselves." (6)

Now, Time for Reader Reflection

The inspirational leader goes beyond having just a focus on driving results and building sustainable growth. They are exceptional communicators, able to enhance personal connections with purpose, and strengthen meaningful relationships. Every leader has their unique style of communicating. They can present and share a clear and compelling vision, connecting a long-term mission with the day-to-day actions. They show openness to feedback and a willingness to listen to the needs of others. They are good observ-ers and they are able to communicate with perspective regarding different situations and challenges.

Leaders need to be able to drive <u>connections</u> way beyond the ar-ticulated facts or messages. They need to reach the hearts and in-ner behaviors of the employee population, helping each individual participate in building the company future as well as in the han-dling of the unforeseen hurdles. Inspiring leaders appreciate the di-versity of experiences and capabilities of their people. They drive a commitment to creativity in thinking and innovation to adapting to changes in the business environment. These leaders make connec-tions utilizing different approaches, such as the sharing of examples and personal experiences.

Leaders evolve <u>relationships</u> into followers and partners based on their excitement and ability to motivate. They demonstrate the value and appreciation for individual differences. They recognize followers as strong challengers and supportive contributors to the organization. These inspiring leaders show comfort with them-selves, accepting their own weaknesses along with strengths, and being willing to be vulnerable. These leaders are real, caring and passionate individuals with an authentic focus on knowing their company people.

The inspiring-communicating leader truly unlocks the inner self of employees. They build understanding with curiosity and compassion. They are able to ignite behavioral change and spur innovative engage-ment with an outstanding vision for the future. They inspire trust and build respect at all levels of the organization. They excite, energize, and engage the entire workforce. They help and support employees to meet their short and long-term goals. They link the multitude of components within the growing and evolving organization.

As per James Kouzes and Barry Posner in the April 2017 Newsletter – The Leadership Challenge (John Wiley & Sons, Inc.) – *"You can't command commitment; you have to inspire it. In these times of rapid change and uncertainty, people want to follow those who can see beyond today's difficulties and imagine a brighter tomorrow."* (7)

Styles of Communication

Leadership communication skills and competencies are based on high-levels of self-awareness, and abilities to strengthen relationships. These capabilities provide insights into how to decrease unnecessary stress and anxiety in life, and to find ways to be more positive with assertive connections. As described in previous chapters, the **Wilson Learning Social Style Model** (8) defines four primary communication styles specific to assertiveness and responsiveness – Driver / Expressive / Amiable / Analytical. Communication versatility by leaders is clearly a challenge and must be driven by personal self-awareness. Creative solutions to difficult problems can be handled through different communication styles.

THE SOCIAL STYLE MODEL

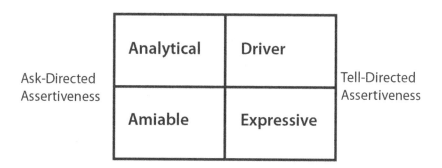

Task-Directed Responsiveness

Ask-Directed Assertiveness

| Analytical | Driver |
| Amiable | Expressive |

Tell-Directed Assertiveness

People-Directed Responsiveness

There are many behavioral aspects that can influence communication styles and the ability to impact others. All leaders need to be adaptive and versatile in connecting with their employee population. They need to be authentic in their messaging and open as well as inclusive in their listening – basically removing preconceived notions and stereotyping. There is a need to balance the message structure with free-flowing information.

Let's look at the four communication styles.

First, if a leader is primarily an <u>analytical</u> communicator, being very task and ask oriented, they are driven by the facts, data and the numbers. They are more logical with their "information" connections and can be perceived as cold as well as overly structured.

Now, as a tell-task <u>driver</u> leader, the communication style can seem more intuitive and big picture oriented. These leaders may seem to lack patience and are seen as fast movers.

In contrast, an <u>amiable</u> leader is more functional by being more ask-assertive and people-directed responsive. These leaders are more methodical and process driven. They are detail gathers and may get bogged down in time lines.

Finally, a more personal communication style is an <u>expressive</u> leader. They are more emotional and connect with others through good listening. Even being tell-directed assertive, the people responsiveness is through feelings and personalization.

Regardless, all leaders need to understand that there are different styles of communication, both by the message provider as well as by the message receiver. Leaders need to be flexible and versatile in their approach to connecting and engaging. In so doing, they can build trust, credibility, and the ability to address organizational challenges.

Leadership Communications from the Head and the Heart

Leaders as connectors, conversationalists and as communicators.

A Personal Story

During the 1990's, I worked for Ohaus Corporation, a manufacturer of weighing equipment for many industries, even mechanical balances used in the chemistry laboratories of high schools. Eventually, Ohaus was acquired by Mettler-Toledo, headquartered in Switzerland, one of the largest weight-measuring manufacturers in the world. Following the merger of Ohaus with Mettler-Toledo, the Ohaus dealer distribution network became concerned that they may not have access to the product lines that they were selling over the past several years.

Well, communications became a critical success factor to continue to drive business growth. Many face-to-face visits, and collaborative discussions regarding product offerings began the steps to successful support and change. All of these contacts were further combined with extensive advertising, new product promotions, and tradeshow customer connections. This impacted the comfort level and confidence with the Ohaus-distribution relationships as partners.

Things continued to evolve during the following months, and years. There were many trips and meetings with the distributors throughout the US. The business distributor-leaders still feared the potential of losing a product line that had been very successful. So, to regain confidence and comfort, the key was the communication and explanation of the new marketing approach based on a dual-brand strategy – the ability to provide both Ohaus balances as well as select Mettler-Toledo products. These personal connections and engagements, as well as active listening to needs and the learning about distributor desires, drove energy and enthusiasm back into the distribution and selling activities. The details on future product offerings and the descriptions on several outstanding advertising campaigns created tremendous excitement about the future relationship and partnerships with Ohaus / Mettler-Toledo. One of the best components was the expansion of the product offerings, along with new balance lines that had the Ohaus "look", yet the technology of the renowned M-T organization.

Through the positive field-based customer relationships activities, there was a move to enhance the internal communications programs with the total employee population. Regular Town Hall meetings occurred. Specific displays of advertising campaign materials as well as new product brochures gained fantastic engagement of the workers at all levels. Everyone felt that they were more collaboratively involved in the many changes as they were happening. They felt a higher level of energy and being valued in the workplace.

Key Discovery... Communicate! Communicate! Communicate!

General Summary on Leadership and Communications from the Head and the Heart

Authentic and effective leadership communication drives employee population connections, and it enhances goal-achievement success levels that can build organizational outcomes and growth.

As per Max de Pree in his book **Leadership is an Art,** *"In most vital organizations, there is a common bond of*

interdependence, mutual interest, interlocking contribu-
tions, and simple joy. Part of the art of leadership is to see
that this common bond is maintained and strengthened, a
task certainly requiring good communication. Just as a re-
lationship requires honest and open communication to stay
healthy, so the relationships within corporations improve
when information is shared accurately and freely." (9)

Closing Thoughts as per the Johari Window (10)

A simple psychological self-discovery and communication model

This model or tool can be used to help drive an understanding specific to interpersonal skills, self-awareness, and ways to improve communications. The Johari Window was created by Joseph Luft and Harry Ingham in 1955 for the purpose of improving personal understanding and individual development. This cognitive model can provide insights and approaches to enhancing relationships, developing teams, and connecting conversations. The key is to always know oneself as well as learn what other people know about you as an individual.

This tool builds on two primary ideas:

1. Building trust with others by disclosing facts about oneself.

2. Learning about oneself via feedback from others, that can help enhance an understanding of personal issues.

As with many learning and development models, there are four quadrants.

The first quadrant is called the open area or free / public area.

- Things one knows about oneself.
- Things others know about you.
- This can be a focus on behaviors, knowledge, skills and attitudes.

The second quadrant is called the blind area or blind spot.

- Things one does not know about oneself.
- Things that are known by others.
- This can be simple or deep issues such as inadequacies.

The third quadrant is called the hidden area or avoided-self area.

- Things one knows about oneself.
- Things not known to others.

The forth quadrant is called the unknown area.

- Things one does not know about oneself.
- Things also unknown by others.

THE JOHARI WINDOW MODEL

	Known by self	Unknown by self
	ASK	
Known by others	1: OPEN AREA	2: BLIND AREA
Tell		
Unknown by others	3: HIDDEN AREA	4: UNKNOWN AREA

Now, use the model to expand the "open area window" and to gain the importance of honest communications.

A. Ask for feedback – this will shrink or reduce the "blind window" as well as the "unknown window". Through self-disclosure and accepting feedback, one can grow personally, and professionally. One can enhance growth areas within one's character.

B. Tell others about oneself – things that may not be known to others – this will shrink the "hidden area window" as well as open the "open area window". Self-exposure and gaining feedback leads to self-discovery and improved communication.

Remember - *Leadership communication and connections come from the head and the heart!*

And, leadership self-awareness is based on human chemistry!

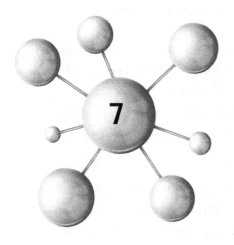

LEADERSHIP AND INTERPERSONAL CONNECTION

Leaders building coaching cultures and active listening environments.

The Chemistry Connection

Chemistry focuses on the understanding of interactions between molecules and on how every interaction can produce changes within our world. A chemical reaction is a process that transforms a substance into another chemical substance. Chemicals are involved in the production of energy, in supporting as well as sustaining our ecosystem, and in mechanism that can even affect climate change. There actually is a need for an evidence-based framework to drive effective chemical connections as well as relationships that can result in desired outcomes.

Leadership coaching along with active listening is also based on interactions and engagement from the human side. It is a process as well as a journey overtime specific to connections and communication, and clearly not just a one-time event. It is the astounding coaching relationships that establishes presence between the coach and the client. It is built on commitment and trust. Exploring and discovering different ways of thinking and dealing with challenges drive leaders to help employees enhance their performance as well as change their personal behaviors. The leadership learning journey for both the leader and the coach-client is a growth path through *human chemistry* that can impact business outcomes and results.

General Remarks on Leadership

Highly engaged employees are emotionally and intellectually committed to deliver strong performance. They take pride in their work as well as in the organization. They are more aligned with the company goals and are willing to exert discretionary effort. An "E Cubed Employee" is an individual who is energetic, enthusiastic and engaged. These employees usually stay with organizations longer and are able to be more creative as well as innovative. Even the quality of their work may be higher, and their personal contributions can even successfully impact the bottom line. All of these factors are driven by effective leaders that are focused on building organizations with an engaging cultural environment. These leaders recognize and reward employee achievements, and they demonstrate a more adaptive willingness to accept dynamic change.

Interpersonal leadership coaching can help drive valuable outcomes, such as an increase in innovative thinking and the enhancement of the ability to handle continuous evolutions within the organization. Coaching leaders can build higher levels of energy and commitment throughout the employee population to the everyday challenges within the company.

As per Frederic Hudson of the Hudson Institute of Santa Barbara, California - *"Coaches anchor people to their own internal strengths; they inspire organizations to dream beyond their plans. They apply emotional and intellectual intelligence to the long haul of life and work."* (1)

Leaders as Coaches

Coaching is a fundamental part of developing the skills of people in an organization so that they have the capacity to solve business problems of today. Coaching is a process of growing key strengths in others and building the capacity to accept the need to bring about change. This competency of coaching vastly increases the ability of the leader to enhance employee performance as well as to enrich personal relationships. Through new and varying approaches within job responsibilities, alternative problem-solving techniques are discovered and learned by the employee coaching-clients. And, these employees are able to identify potential opportunities so that they can continue to become more engaged and to be stronger contributors to the organization.

The leader-coaching process helps employees become more capable and versatile, encouraging them to grow into action-oriented business drivers. There are four components in an effective and value-focused coaching-client engagement.

First, the coach **builds the connection**. They establish the foundation based on trust, values, and respect. They certainly do not connect or act as counselors or therapist. Rather, they are enhancing the relationship through formal and informal activities and communication sessions.

Second, the coach **establishes the required commitment** by the client to the process. They focus initially on the desired goals and outcomes. They motivate by getting all discussions in-sync with specific needs and desires. Strong active listening and gaining insights through carefully composed questioning becomes the drivers of the one-on-one meetings.

Third, the coach helps the client **grow new capabilities.** There is a self-reflection process that drives self-discoveries. As part of this learning journey, new competencies and capabilities are found and grown. The coach encourages the application and utilization of the newly discovered skills.

Forth, the coach takes time to **provide recognition.** They acknowledge successes and specific achievements. Challenges that are identified are carefully reviewed to help the client move onto new changes and approaches. There is the use of positive as well as constructive feedback, and the sharing of insights to help build confidence for the future.

Active listening (as described in earlier chapters) is part of the leader-coaching process. It is a special art and a craft based on human connections and *human chemistry*. It is an approach that removes filters and judgements, and builds self-awareness and deeper personal understanding. This competency of active listening is based on seeking real insights and not on just mentally preparing a reply. It is driven by developing complete context and being fully present. It involves both the mind and the body. The mind needs to be open, looking for the central theme and analyzing what is being said as well as not being said. The body requires eye contact, watching for non-verbal signs, and using care by the leader-coach not to over interrupt what is being shared. The leader must develop true engagement with the client and make connections from the heart.

The active listening process is based on personal self-awareness by the leader. Yes, the overall goal is to enhance productivity, and learn how to improve the ability to influence as well as to persuade and negotiate. Again, this listening skill can be organized into a four-step approach that is very similar to the leader-coaching process.

First, the coach-leader must develop the **listening connection**. By giving attention to the client, the leader acknowledges the message and content of the discussion. Key is not to become distracted mentally or by the surrounding environment. Always take note of the body language and the non-verbal communication.

Second, the coach must **demonstrate the connection** with the client. They may let their face do some of the communicating, and once again, provide encouragement through acknowledgement and confirmation of the discussion content. The coach can even use their own posture and body language to confirm the connection.

Third, there is a point reached for **reflective sharing.** The coach can paraphrase the understanding of the message and continue to ask more in-depth questions. The coach always tries to remove assumptions and conclusions, and never shows judgment. Without interrupting, summarizing on occasional can drive additional understanding and focus.

Forth, a new level of sharing is reached called **responsive connecting.** The relationship of the coach and the client reach new levels of trust and openness. Both are very honest and respectful. There is a sharing of opinions and as well as discussions on possible potential options for the future and ways to tackle unknown challenges.

Being an active listener requires work. And, each leader has a different listening style and approach since it is based on an internal process. Good listening skills are established on the ability to ask the right questions at the right time. In summary.............

> Physically – face the speaker and maintain eye contact
> Physically – lean toward the speaker yet stay relaxed
> Physically – watch for non-verbal signs and do not interrupt
> Mentally – listen for the central theme and keep an open mind
> Mentally – analyze what is being said
> Mentally – listen to what is not being said

The leader must be aware that everyone they are connecting with will have different listening preferences, such as a focus on content and data, versus on people and emotions. Time availability along with actual time pressures can even impact the quality of the active listening interactions.

So, when is a leader a coach and an active listener? When they become positive and trusted change-agents. They have learned how to drive the abilities of people to sustain motivation and commitment to the long-term projects as well as the strategic vision of the future business. They are able to enhance collaboration and handle conflicts by carefully balancing priorities, purpose and planning. The ego of the leader must not interfere with the growth of quality relationships. Actually, the values and beliefs of the leader must become fully connected to the organizational structure and company culture.

Leaders as coaches and as active listeners must have the internal strengths to be change-agents so that they can encourage the employee population of an organization to question the status quo and to be willing to challenge the unknown. They accept in others risk-taking, mistakes, and different perspectives to issues and processes, yet, as leaders, they must always remain optimistic about future results. Through personal self-confidence, this change-agent leader is able to listen intently from the heart, and show caring behaviors that are natural and real. Giving constructive criticism is achieved through accuracy of content and a fairness with all forms of feedback, both positive as well as constructive. The plans and established goals of the leader can be achieved through their personal integrity and an inspired workforce.

Based on vast experiences and knowledge from the work-world, the leader-listener-coach will have developed a strong personal self-awareness. They have a true focus on the company and their employees, versus just on their own personal needs. They have a strong passion for their business, along with a special intuitive ability to remove barriers that could stand in the way of success. These leaders build teams, both with direct reports as well as with indirect individuals, that can be successful and have a feeling of appreciation, always helping each team member find fulfillment with their work responsibilities. This type of leader drives engagement and commitment resulting in employees that always seems to go beyond their personal limitations and that go the extra mile for the organization. These team-oriented employees have a purpose which is fully aligned with the business mission. Their achievements can go beyond their potentials, resulting in a higher level of life satisfaction. Why? Because coaching-listening-leaders are well connected to their people. They demonstrate authentic and inspiring leadership competencies. They are always utilizing *human chemistry* to build partnerships.

The GROW Model

Leaders as coaches have opportunities to drive organizational productivity and enhance the quality of the work environment.

They clearly can impact overall communication and improve business interpersonal relationships. Using a model can provide the structure to deepen the coaching experience and build even stronger desired behaviors. The four-stage GROW Model (2) is a very widely used approach in the coaching conversation. Also recognized as part of decision-making skills, goal-setting and problem-solving activities, the GROW model and process was developed by Graham Alexander, Sir John Whitmore and colleagues in the UK during the end of 1980s. It was first published in Whitmore's book – *Coaching for Performance*. (3)

The GROW Model is great with coaching conversations and also a powerful leadership tool based on its flexibility. Leaders as coaches are always inspiring and driving client aspirations into actions so that they can achieve personal as well as professional goals.

The four stages of the model are as follows.

G – Goal – "What do you want?"

Key is to establish what the client or coachee wants to achieve at the outset of the coaching engagement. This is the purpose of the coach-client relationship and creates a focus on the potential "big picture" regarding the business and optional actions. Personal improvements will occur along with the actual influencing of the client. Defining achievements should be specific and clear.

R – Reality – "Where are you now?"

Understanding where the client is currently and how the client is progressing toward the established goals are important. Are they clear on their current abilities and knowledge to meet the goals? The coach can help the client better understand their own attributes and strengths, and build an awareness of opportunities for personal growth and development. Additionally, aspects of reality can be found specific to the challenges and issues associated with the reaching of the goals.

<u>O – Options – "What could you do?"</u>

The coach helps the client explore options and the possibilities for learning new ideas and strategies. Obstacles can be identified and ways to deal with these challenges can be addressed. Key is getting a handle on time constraints, cost impacts, and risks associated with choices.

<u>W – Will / Wrap-Up – "What will you do?"</u>

This coaching model can always provide space to look back at any of the stages throughout the process and the coach-client relationship. It is driven by the client. Specific action steps helps move the client toward the meeting of the established goals and fully commits to new steps going forward.

This framework is based on the needs of the client throughout the conversation. Coaching can transform individuals and build their personal awareness along with the unlocking of their confidence and the finding of specific motivators. Coaching is a powerful way to change behaviors and enhance the abilities of individuals to impact business results as well as personal achievements.

Personal Story - Leadership and Coaching

During my career with Ohaus Corporation (US) / Mettler-Toledo (Switzerland), an opportunity surfaced by moving from a marketing leadership role into a human resource position, as described in the previous chapter. This HR career step further evolved by joining Datascope Corp. (US) as the head of human resources for the Cardiac Assist Division, reporting to the Corporate Officer of HR, and having a dotted-line relationship to my primary customer, the CEO for the CA Division. Over the following years at Datascope, additional opportunities and new responsibilities surfaced. I fully enjoyed my work and I believe that I had an excellent impact on many organizational successes as well as on the employee population, building exceptional relationships at all levels of the company.

With the desire to continue to learn and grow as an individual as well as a leader, and by having a deep interest to embrace my value-oriented position at Datascope, I assembled a business proposal based on the potential of influencing and driving behavioral changes within management. This clearly would be a process of impacting a cultural evolution. And, this would be accomplished by developing a "learning-business-world" specific to a rigorous internally-based coaching mindset and skill growth capability. The overall purpose would be to improve organizational effectiveness and business outcomes through coaching-oriented leaders. The proposal was presented, reviewed and accepted by the senior leadership group. The next step was to become a certified executive-career/life coach through a demanding and engaging experience provided by the Hudson Institute of Santa Barbara in California. It was almost a full-year learning journey, and there were many challenges and hurdles specific to my current commitments and responsibilities at Datascope.

The project vision was clear. First - To gain my coaching certification through the acceptance by the company for time commitment requirements along with the funding of this initiative. Second - To create and implement development activities throughout Datascope that could evolve into a holistic coaching mindset and culture. This could result in a dramatic organizational transformation.

The overall objective of this business initiative would be a reformulation of the organization's link to behavioral changes by the company population specific to personal growth and development of all leaders and employees. Everyone would develop new competencies and be able to establish a stronger connection between their work and life. The initial impact would focus on changing behaviors in managers, and eventually overtime, there would be a transformation in the overall culture at Datascope.

This engaging and interactive culture would drive business effectiveness resulting in an enhancement of performance results. Well, I achieved my certification and underwent several major personal discoveries. Unfortunately, the total implementation of the business initiative was not realized. Datascope Corp. began selling off one of the major divisions, and eventually, sold the final business components to another medical device organization in Germany (Maquet Medical Systems), that was part of a larger organization in Sweden (The Getinge Group).

Of course, a full review of this exciting initiative can provide excellent insights into the potential impact a coaching-mindset would have on an organization as well as on the entire employee population involved in any transformation. Internally, one-on-one coaching occurred, giving several managers an understanding and buy-in to the coaching-learning process. The development of coaching skills by managers would become a strategic and long-term approach to managing and leading others. It would be more than just a one-time event or a simple managerial technique, but a way of adding value for all employees, driving growth under a clear coaching focus and management style. This coaching-mindset, without a doubt, would potentially impact the bottom line and profitability of the organization.

This long-term business initiative would take place over several years, yet many outcomes for the company and its employees would be realized in shorter windows of time.

- Managers and their direct reports would confront work and life with different perspectives.
- Employees would develop new skills and increase their abilities to undergo personal self-reflection and discoveries.
- Managers would drive new levels of relationships and become stronger leaders in their roles. They would become more successful in surfacing critical issues and on holding crucial conversations. They would be better at managing challenging confrontations.
- Employees would develop higher levels of trust in leaders, and even be more comfortable taking risks and being more innovative. They would grow and learn through positive and constructive feedback.
- All employees would feel committed and involved in driving strategic plans into actions and results. They would also be enhancing their problem-solving skills.
- Coaching would become the language for managerial communications and connections. It would become the foundation of all learning and development, as well as part of performance management system and succession planning processes.

- Coaching would drive the need for active listening in all performance discussions.

The coaching-mindset would help build a stronger and healthier organization, from the top down as well as from the bottom up. The "efficient and effective" company would undergo a continuous change process along with a focus on learning and development of skills and competencies.

> As per Marshall Goldsmith, Laurence Lyons, and Alyssa Freas in their book entitled **Coaching for Leadership – How the World's Greatest Coaches Help Leaders Learn,** *"Language is not the only thing changing. The perspective is shifting steadily and surely from labor to knowledge; from management to leadership; from product to customers and service; from routine operation to inspired creativity; and from task repetition to marketing innovation. As technology and automation shift the boredom of work from people to machines, the human world of work that remains challenges our intellect, not our muscle."* (4)

The transformational process would focus on five key areas.

#1 A cultural mindset transformation!

The process would open the door to a new cultural mindset. It would start first with managers, who have the greatest impact on their direct reports. Managers would help all employees become more introspective. Individuals would work in an environment which would encourage creative ideas and unique solutions to problems. Employees would develop new perspectives on their work activities and personal lives. They would be more involved in their careers versus just performing a job. They would be more engaged and productive, and improvement in morale and commitment to the organization would result in higher levels of retention.

#2 A leadership transformation!

The process would push managers at all levels and in different positions to continue to reach new levels of greatness. Employees would be more motivated, achieve higher levels of individual satisfaction, and find greater successes from their job. Again, this would clearly impact productivity and retention.

> As per Jim Collins in his book - **Good to Great – Why Some Companies Make the Leap...and others Don't** - leadership greatness *"is the quiet, deliberate process of pushing on the fly wheel to produce results".* *"Disciplined action, following from disciplined people who exercise disciplined thoughts."* (5)

#3 A team transformation!

The process would help encourage and build better working relationships and team connections. Employees would become stronger business partners with each other, working more successfully and drawing improvements in overall effectiveness and operational productivity.

> Again, Jim Collins states in his book - **Good to Great** - *"the people from good-to-great companies clearly love what they did, largely because they loved who they did it with".* (6)

#4 A coaching skills transformation!

The process would build stronger leaders as well as develop managers into leaders by using a coaching language along with coaching skills. Managers would move from a focus on short-term goals and tactical activities to a more long-term mission and strategic approach to leading. They would move away from rigid and controlling behaviors, to ones that are more inspiring and future focused, as well as more enriched with delegation and empowerment. They would learn to have higher levels of flexibility and to promote a sense of individual self-worth.

> Again, Jim Collins states – *"One needs to create a climate where the truth is heard."* (7)

He recommends four practices:

1. Lead with questions, not answers.

2. Engage in dialogue and debate, not coercion.

3. Conduct autopsies, without blame – always search for understanding and learning.

4. Build red flag mechanisms – turning information into information that cannot be ignored.

Most of these leadership behaviors would come from five well-defined and crafted learning and development modules as well as from on-the-job practices and applications. This would be a continuous process based on the desire to embrace self-growth and personal learning, versus just a burst of short-term training. A more real and authentic leadership style would begin to surface due to the new coaching-skill strengths and the abilities to influence behaviors from the heart. Once again, there would be an impact on overall company performance.

#5 A modeling-the-way transformation

The process would have all managers, now behaving more like leaders, and leaders being seen as true leaders, all because they are modeling coaching behaviors and methods of communication. They would be able to motivate direct reports to more sustainable levels. This would, once again, lead to enhance employee commitment, especially toward long-term strategies. New behaviors of collaboration, engagement, risk-taking, and being more action-oriented would help to continue to build a more positive work environment. There would be higher levels of job enjoyment and fun at work. The one-on-one coaching along with regular feedback would enhance individual self-awareness. The blending of cognitive learning via the actual doing, would result in a learning and development culture based on coaching. Practice leads to absorption. New hires would be more likely to adapt to this type of culture and become rapidly more productive contributors in their roles.

The background rationale and research for this business initiative was based on specific survey data regarding the use of coaching, including the key skill of active listening. Here are a few interesting points. The survey was presented at the HRD 2006 Learning and Development Conference in London. It was based on an article that appeared in **Coaching at Work** magazine (March/April Issue) (8) that was produced on behalf of the Chartered Institute of Personnel and Development, London, UK. (9) They stated that companies are aspiring to have a coaching culture and believe it is a main driver for improving the performance of employees and the business. The key survey findings were as follows:

> ➤ *Four out of five organizations (79%) now use coaching as part of their effort to develop their people.*
> ➤ *Eighty percent of those using coaching state that their organizations aspire to having a coaching culture and 75% say they are investing time and resources to achieve this aim.*
> ➤ *Fifty-three percent of organizations using coaching employ dedicated internal and external coaches for this purpose.*

> *The most popular means by which coaching is delivered is via the training of the line managers to fulfill this role. Four-fifths (82%) of the organizations using coaching train line managers to act as coaches, and for nearly half (47%) this is the only means by which they deliver coaching.*
> *Sixty nine percent of organizations say coaches they use are not accredited, certified or licensed.*

Right Management (10), a consulting organization, together with Manchester Consulting (11), conducted studies regarding the use of coaching across a variety of roles and levels, verifying the value of investing in internal coaching programs and in creating a coaching culture. Coaching recipients were highly satisfied by their experience. Many goals were met, including interpersonal improvements, better management and leadership skills, business agility, and personal growth.

Source - ***Coaching Executive Summary – What's the Quantifiable Return on Investment – 2004*** – Right Management Consultants, Philadelphia, PA. (12)

Tangible business results were as follows:

- *Improved productivity (53%); Better quality (48%);*
- *Greater organizational strength (48%)*
- *Better customer service (39%); Reduced customer complaints (34%);*
- *Improved retention (32%)*
- *Cost reductions (23%); Better bottom line profitability (22%)*
- *Top line revenue growth (14%); Reduced turnover (12%)*

Intangible business results were as follows:

- *Better relationships with direct reports (77%);*
- *Better relationships with supervisors (71%)*
- *Improved teamwork (67%); Better relationships with peers (63%);*
- *Greater job satisfaction (61%)*
- *Reduced conflict (52%); improved organizational commitment (44%)*
- *Better relationships with customers (37%)*

The Datascope business initiative had several well-defined key success factors.

- ❖ Have a very well planned and deliberate approach to the coaching activities and total initiative.

  - o Use a systematic approach.

  - o Provide development at a high-quality level.

- ❖ Have a very well defined coaching process and a centralized learning structure.

  - o Clear goals for organizational learning.

  - o Clear expectations for the one-on-one interventions.

- ❖ Have the coaching initiative drive changes in behaviors.

  - o Let the culture change flow.

- ❖ Have coaches that are appropriately trained on the use of various learning methodologies and are focused on a limited set of goals.

  - o It is in-sync and consistent with business strategies.

- ❖ Have the coaching initiative a total company project.

  - ○ It needs to be understood by the organization.

  - ○ It needs top level support and buy-in.

- ❖ Have an established level of accountability of the coaching process.

  - ○ Penetrate the organization at the middle management level.

- ❖ Have the coaching competencies as an integral part of the leadership development strategy.

  - ○ It complements the leadership model.

  - ○ It is marketed as a positive, development activity and growth strategy.

The Value of a Coaching Culture Initiative

The Center for Effective Organizations, Marshall School of Business at the University of Southern California (13), and Capital One Financial Service (14), conducted an extensive survey to measure the organizational impact of coaching.

> Two key conclusions were reached (as documented in the Journal of the Human Resource Planning Society – Volume 30 / Issue 2 – 2007 – "What Coaching Can and Cannot Do for Your Organization"). (15)

> 1. Greater use of internal coaches is associated with improved team and strategic execution at management

levels throughout the organization – high, medium and low.

2.   More internal coaching for middle managers appears to improve culture and morale.

The research defined coaching as one-on-one interventions and issues associated with job related decision-making and actions. The downside to the investigation, which involved 55 large companies, was that the data was conducted on-line (self-reports) and the usual respondent was the person responsible for coaching initiatives. There could be some bias toward the positive coaching impact. Some skepticism also surfaced based on the disorganized approach used in the internal coaching.

- Top level impact and positive outcome specific to coaching was in areas of developing future leaders, and improving behaviors and individual employee's performance.
- Other areas of impact included strategy execution, teamwork, change management, perceived responsiveness of management, employee motivation, and organization culture and values.

The research indicated that coaching clearly improved an organization's effectiveness. The growth of a richer talent pool helped better equip leaders driving organizational performance, developed successors for leaders, and improved the overall career learnings.

Three clear patterns emerged when comparing organizations using coaching versus organizations using coaching less extensively.

First, there was an impact on strategy and teamwork.

- Improvements were found in the following areas:

    o Ability to execute business strategy

    o Alignment and teamwork among the senior leaders

    o Teamwork at levels below the senior level

Second, there was an impact on employee motivation and organization culture.

- Improvements were found in the following areas:

    o Engagement of employees at all levels

    o Organizational values

Third, there was an impact on communication and perceived responsibilities of management.

- Improvement were found in the following areas:

    o Management is responsive to workplace issues

    o Key communication of important and sensitive messages

Final Thoughts

All coaching engagements and initiatives need to be carefully coordinated. A disciplined approach helps drive the overall effectiveness of the business initiative. Internal coaching helps improve teamwork and strategy execution at all management levels throughout the organization. Targeting internal coaching at middle managers can pay-off in terms of improved culture and morale. And, building a coaching business environment and a coaching organizational culture, must including the key coaching component of active listening. This clearly would impact organizational effectiveness.

As per an article written by Aria de Geus – **Planning as Learning** (Harvard Business Review – March/ April 1988 issue)........*learning and building a coaching culture, supported by leadership energy, agility and resilience. Coaching and active listening is a language and they are communication-connecting tools.* De Geus is a business executive for Shell Oil Company, and also a well-known business theorist.

"When people play (mental models of the world), they are actually creating a new language among themselves that expresses the knowledge they have acquired. And here we come to the most important aspect of institutional learning, whether it be achieved through teaching or through play as we have defined: the institutional learning process is a process of language development. As the implicit knowledge of each of each learner becomes explicit, his or her mental model becomes a building block of the institutional model. How much and how fast this model changes will depend on the culture and structure of the organization. Teams that have to cope with rigid procedures and information systems will learn more slowly than those with flexible, open communication channels. Auto-critic institutions will learn faster or not at all – the ability of one or a few leaders being a risky institutional bet." (16)

Building a rigorous internal coaching-mindset and driving behavioral changes are clearly challenging business initiatives. Creating this holistic coaching mindset is based on adult learning over time and based on growth with value to the participants. Company and leadership commitment to this process needs to focus on several strategic learning modules as part of the learning journey. The personal mastery of the techniques will not occur over night.

Here are some examples of learning modules.

- Manager as Leader – The evolution of coaching and the holistic coaching model
- Becoming an Active Listener – Building a relationship by asking versus telling
- Dealing with Challenges and Change – Pushing past resistance and supporting change
- Moving Plans into Actions – Effectively implementing goals and strategies into actions
- Creating Team-Oriented Coaching – Building partnerships and driving behavioral changes

Coaching-listening-leaders are well connected to their people and demonstrate authentic and inspiring leadership competencies. They are always utilizing *human chemistry.*

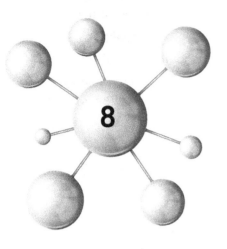

LEADERSHIP AND BUSINESS KNOWLEDGE / CAPABILITIES

Leaders enhancing employee engagement through different leadership styles.

The Chemistry Connection

Chemical reactions are either exothermic or endothermic and are opposite with regards to reaction energy. Exothermic reactions release energy in the form of heat or light, resulting in negative enthalpy change. Endothermic reactions absorb energy to complete the reaction, resulting in positive enthalpy change. The key difference is that the end products of exothermic reactions are more stable than endothermic reactions that are less stable due to weaker chemical bonds.

Leaders need to find ways to release energy within the employee population and to build bonds between team members that are stable and value oriented. As we all know, group "reactions" can have both negative and positive outcomes. Building relationships, partnerships, and insights into personal self-awareness will need to continue to be developed by leaders. Specifically, the focus must be on critical thinking abilities and many soft-skills, such as emotional intelligence, collaboration, and time as well as conflict management. Leaders need to have courage and confidence in their decision-making and risk-taking activities. The *human chemistry* of leadership is using the heart, the body, and the mind to getting things done, making action-oriented contributions, and accomplishing inspiring goals. And, it is the end-result that is critical in building organizational engagement along with long-term growth and successes.

General Remarks on Leadership

Looking back at previous thoughts and insights on leadership capabilities, here is a quick review of the competencies of leaders in a structure that is based on three categories. They are grouped under two skill areas.

> Hard skills are the "what" capabilities specific to *business knowledge and technical skills* (Category One). These are cognitive abilities. They are focused on in-depth business understanding and the mastery of managerial as well as administrative activities in a professional and insightful manner. Hard skills are developed based on *experiences and capabilities* (Category Two) that are learned during the career journey of the leader.

> Soft skills are the "how" capabilities specific to many abilities, such as active listening, influencing with inspiration,

dynamically communicating, and demonstrating confidence as well as self-awareness. These are the human and people connecting skills, specifically *behavioral competencies* (Category Three) that are based on personal actions and on establishing expected standards of conduct.

Effective leaders need to think and act globally, as well as be adaptive to constant change in a fast-paced, competitive business environment. These leaders must keep growing new hard skills and knowledge proficiency abilities, especially social character traits and interpersonal communication capabilities. Leadership is an art, a science, a craft, and a critical ability to focus on people

During 2011, a consulting organization – DDI - Development Dimensions International in Pittsburgh, Pennsylvania (1) – conducted a creative study and published the following interesting findings in the Wall Street Journal. They identified eight strength-oriented leadership competencies, as well as identified the three top management skills.

> *#1 Setting work standards and taking ownership*
>
> *#2 Planning and organizing*
>
> *#3 Decision making and driving results.*

They also identified the three top skills having the greatest opportunity for development.

> *#1 Delegating and motivating*
>
> *#2 Gaining commitment and strategic focus*
>
> *#3 Listening, coaching, and working with people*

The two of the eight competencies that did not fall into the top two rating groups, either as a strength or a potential for development were:

- *Taking action and communicating*
- *Adaptability and driving innovation*

Ultimately, a leader must use their strengths and competencies as well as knowledge and experiences to influence others and to drive business actions. By taking personal ownership, the goal of the leader is to increase effectiveness of the organization, along with the ability to contribute to the company as a key driver. They must always inspire, motivate, direct and guide actions, and keep leveraging their leadership capabilities and practices. Leaders need to be innovative in nature, strategically focused, results oriented, and capable of communicating a vision for the future. One must accept the fact that leaders have different leadership styles of driving business performance and employee engagement. Yet, all leaders are always focused on people and the *human chemistry*.

Business Acumen / Leadership Styles / Employee Engagement

Leaders take risks every day and pursue business opportunities that can improve organizational financial performance. Having a clear vision and a focus on strategies to drive the "big picture", there are many critical pieces to executive thinking and creative leadership. Without a doubt, these authentic and passionate leaders need to be innovative individuals that work and lead with total conviction and commitment. Their approach to company communication, having a personal and compelling leadership style, utilizing an inclusive decision-making behavior, and driving a strategic action-oriented partnership – all serve as the foundation for leaders to effectively engage with employees and other executives at multiple levels. Relationships, business acumen, and leadership development are

144

also key components for building strong performance management activities that can impact profitability and growth.

Throughout the following pages, we will examine three leadership success factors – business acumen, personal leadership styles, and employee engagement.

<u>Success Factor One - Business Acumen</u>

Even though a leader brings a strong and seasoned level of business knowledge to their leadership position as a result of education and experiences, the business acumen of the leader must continue to be developed and grown over time. It is an important competency and a critical success factor in the leadership learning journey throughout the career of a leader. Building an evolving business mindset along with technical knowledge can help the leader manage and guide challenging situations that can represent opportunities as well as possible risks with value. They need to be able to handle difficult decisions and be accountable during a business environment known today as "VUCA" – volatile, uncertain, complex, and ambiguous.

Leaders are dealing with greater levels of globalization, with an evolving and more fluid workforce, and with diverse electronic communication methodologies, including social media. To build the competitive advantage of an organization, a leader must keep growing their personal business acumen. Several areas require maximum focus by the leader to become more successful and to create a company that is viewed as a premium place to work. Building personal presence and *human chemistry* along with excellent business insights and savvy, drives the ability of a leader to enhance employee trust, teamwork, and overall internal company enthusiasm.

Leaders need to have ....

- ❖ a strong handle on the *big picture and desired outcomes.* A dynamic and clear vision and mission statement can be very inspirational and even able to enhance employee engagement so that outstanding results can be achieved.
- ❖ very powerful and measurable *financial objectives* specific to annual targets as well as to three-year and five-year growth potentials.
- ❖ well defined *cultural values* that can create an aligned and effective workforce. Strong core values can impact employee behavioral collaboration and innovation.
- ❖ specific *communication processes* to drive messages regarding actions, decisions, measures, and successes. Ideas need to be shared openly and able to flow to employees, to managers/executives, and to the customer base.
- ❖ a systematic approach to establishing *business priorities and performance indicators.*
- ❖ clarity of *purpose* to push strategic execution of organizational processes and integrated systems to build competitive marketing advantages. This will drive shareholder wealth and maximize profits.
- ❖ meaningful *behaviors and strong political savvy.*

Business acumen is a learned skill – acquired on the job, from formal educational programs, through mentorship and coaching, and via specific activities that occur both internal and external to the organization. The personal growth of a leader clearly impacts their psychological make-up and thought processes. This growth dynamic is based on a combination of factors or development approaches as part of the leadership learning journey.

- The leader can undergo business simulations to help with making decisions and analyzing real-life situations. Mistakes can even become learning events.
- Job roles can be changes via rotations or even foreign assignments abroad to enhance multicultural perspectives as well as global awareness.
- University programs or internally developed long-term learning events can provide impact through higher levels of flexibility and adaptability.
- Learning & Development consultants can custom-craft programs and workshops that target specific business learning needs.
- Teamwork and connections across multiple company areas can help incorporate the learnings.
- Executive coaching can be utilized to enhance the on-the-job application and utilization of the learnings.

Actually, business acumen goes way beyond business knowledge, past experiences, and analytical thinking. Therefore, the leadership learning journey must fully support the individual's development of broader, more in-depth mental insights and incredible self-discoveries. As responsibilities of the leader increase, the acumen competencies will also need to grow and expand. Ultimately, the leader becomes more effective in decision-making and problem-solving, and in risk-taking and execution of actions. They are able to drive more agile and higher-performing teams and groups based on personal self-confidence along with their acceptance of vulnerability.

<u>Success Factor Two - Personal Leadership Styles</u>

Effective leaders inspire workplace commitment and drive sustainable performance outcomes. They focus on high standards, build respect and trust, and always express thanks and appreciation for exceptional contributions. Successful leaders are open and transparent, clearly self-aware, and willing to take risks and be vulnerable. Based on past business experiences, learning activities, and personal self-discoveries, leaders have developed their own capabilities, behaviors, and personalities to lead. They have different styles of leadership, different ways of demonstrating passion and commitment, and diverse ways of driving their personal presence within an organization. Their skills and characteristics are clearly situational and may vary based on the challenges that they are facing on a daily basis. Yet, several styles and performance leadership competencies are core to the specific individual as a leader. And, truly successful leaders have learned to shift from one leadership style to another based on the circumstantial demands. They have found ways to be flexible and to balance their primary leadership style with secondary styles.

Leadership is a complex and self-discovery process. All engagements, connections, and relationships are based on the challenges and specific situations that a leader needs to address. The thinking activities and behaviors of leaders are enhanced by the required accountability as well as issues associated with business transformations and desired results. The approach to leading and managing is established by the use of winning attributes and attitudes with a focus on successful outcomes. So, primary leadership styles are the drivers with secondary styles serving as backup. Effective leadership is always based on critical competencies and capabilities – the ability to manage change, build relationships, inspire others, maintain agility, and to gain decisive strategic perspectives.

Leadership styles can be grouped into <u>eight different categories</u>, all evolving from a leader's imagination, creativity, strategies, confidence, and personal boundaries. And, the characteristics of being an effective and influencing leader are based on their individual

148

strengths, ambition, persistence, and behavioral courage. As already stated, leaders have preferred leadership styles, yet are able to move to a different style based on situations or challenges. So, the selected style is driven by acquired attributes and comfort, and by the real-world that the leader is operating within specific to their organization.

Pacesetting / Autocratic Style – leaders that have high standards for themselves and others, and have a focus on high speed achievement.

> These leaders are very achievement oriented, action driven, and focused primarily on results. Their support teams need to be self-motivated and skilled, and they need to be able to self-direct. Innovation may be squelched, especially when the leader seeks little input from others. The vision could be unclear at times as a result of a closed mindedness and a need only for one way communication. These task-oriented autocrats can destroy commitment and impact the trust of followers. Yet, these pacesetting leaders can actually be nice and decent individuals, even though quick results take precedence over morale.

Democratic / Participative Style – leaders that are very collaborative with decision-making, and have a focus on inspiring commitments into actions.

> These leaders are consensus builders that are able to gain genuine participation along with engaging discussions. Teamwork is clearly focused to enhance ownership and trust in an inspiring vision. Commitment is a key component of the leadership activities, resulting in a strong passion for problem-solving and issue resolutions. Everyone is encouraged by this style of leader to practice consultative

participation and to own their decision consequences. Relationships are enhanced by the democratic leader by gaining input and opinions from all team members. Rapid actions may not always be an outcome, yet the collaborative and supportive behaviors help build inspiration and drive commitment.

People-Focused / Affiliative – leaders that value harmony and emotions, and have a strong focus on people and relationships.

These leaders establish positive relationships based on loyalty and trust as well as through open sharing of ideas and valued feedback. People come first by these leaders, enhancing emotional bonds and strong feelings of belonging. Team harmony, a high level of tolerance, and true empathy all help drive performance and a people-focused work environment, especially without being advice oriented.

Authoritative / Command & Control – leaders that are task-oriented and enthusiastic about a common vision, and have a strong focus on policies and procedures.

These leaders can be autocratic yet always enthusiastic about a common vision and specific targeted goals. They can be seen as extremely controlling on decision-making and even somewhat dictatorial in nature. These leaders are clearly more tell-oriented, inflexible, and drivers of their own ideas and choices. Team member may not feel fully trusted, and their creativity can get stifled. Poor listening and leadership dominance defines this command and control style. Unfortunately, this can result in a division of the authoritative leader and their followers.

Excellent-Focused / Coercive – leaders that are demanding and top-down, and usually have a focus on driving solutions during crisis periods.

> These leaders are also tell-oriented and expect immediate compliance and obedience to the defined expectations. Success is critical to these leaders, yet contrary opinions are drivers of alienation of team members. A lack of flexibility and a strong focus on perfection can make these coercive leaders rule by fear.

Innovative / Transformational – leaders that are driving creativity and an inspiring vision, and have a focus on unlocking tangible values as the foundation for the organization.

> These leaders are very forward looking, addressing challenges and taking risks. There is a high commitment and level of optimism for creative ideas and for pursuing the values of strategic concepts that have purpose. Improving changes within the organization and management can help impact relationships and product improvements. Hopes, values, and needs are driven by innovative leaders into a creative vision with a dream-oriented and dynamic transformation.

Charismatic / Persuasive-Influencer – leaders that are very passionate about success and have a focus on encouraging risk-taking that can influence and impact outcomes.

> These leaders are strong influencers of team members and have high levels of energy and enthusiasm for their leadership roles. By walking-the-talk with integrity and honesty, they are modeling strong behaviors of commitment. Charismatic leaders are able to motivate and inspire, resulting in positive cultures and outstanding work environments.

There is a high level of morale along with ownership and accountability. These leaders have the charm and persuasiveness to enhance unwavering commitment to positive change and to transformational actions.

Coaching / Development-Oriented – leaders that are self-aware and full of empathy, and have a focus on developing employees and colleagues for the future.

These leaders are very learning and development oriented, implementing changes, and helping individuals grow throughout their careers. They are focused on recognizing talent and cultivating new skills. As coaching leaders, they are good active listeners and able to encourage different approaches to problem-solving and decision-making activities. Development leaders build strong and engaging teams, utilizing their foundation of self-awareness.

Leadership is based on the ability to influence and impact an organization in an inspirational way. It is an art, a science, and a craft. It is founded on *human chemistry*. Regardless of an individual's leadership style, all leaders need to be active listeners, to be open and authentic, and to be builders of trust. They need to be present, to be role models, and to be themselves.

As per Jorge Cuervo in his book entitled **Leaders Don't Command,** he states that: *"The systemic function of leadership is to make members of the team resonate along a longitudinal wavelength to boost them toward a common goal, fostering the growth of synergies and creativity. To harmonize people in a human system you need to focus attention on the relationships between them: First you need to build them or, if they already exist, fortify them." (2)*

152

Success Factor Three - Employee Engagement

Employee engagement is a critical component that can drive the successes of the performance of an organization and its business outcomes. An employee that is satisfied with their job can be understood by measuring their personal motivation, their enthusiasm and passion for the company, and their commitment to support management strategies. The feeling and belief that the contributions made by an employee are valued and appreciated clearly will impact the levels of employee retention and turnover.

Employee engagement is an emotional aspect that drives loyalty of an employee as well as their involvement in the success of the company. Leaders need to connect and understand their workforce make-up, and have a willingness to build on employee differences along with individual potentials. By identifying various challenges and finding ways to navigate through business dilemmas, leaders can grow the talent of the organization as well as their own personal capabilities. Leaders are the drivers of relationships and creators of engagement by establishing a culture of openness, trust, and respect. This type of culture helps employees become emotionally connected to their jobs and to the organization. So, employee engagement actually starts with the leader.

Learning about employee satisfaction and depth of engagement can be done through a survey discovery process. This requires the company to carefully defining employee engagement success factors. They will serve as the foundation to building a stronger value-oriented culture.

- The survey execution and data assessment require the identification and selection of a support consulting organization as a partner to help drive all of the related activities.

- The survey must be carefully aligned with the company goals and strategies. There needs to be collaboration between the survey team drivers and the executive leaders that own the critical elements of the business long-term objectives.
- The survey input must be fully analyzed so that robust insights can be discovered for growth steps to be taken going forward. The analysis can help correlate positive employee engagement with specific business outcomes.
- The survey conclusions need to be assembled into a well-defined action plan. These potential improvement activities are prioritized so that the implementation of the specific actions can influence meaningful and measurable changes. Employees become motivated and passionate about potential changes, along with emotional factors that are intrinsically connected to the company.
- The survey actions need to be openly communicated with a focus on clear expectations and on the potential of affecting positive change. Time and resources must be devoted to the distribution of the findings as well as to the action plans for all managers, especially the top leaders. Care needs to be applied in the communication process regarding geography and language barriers.
- The survey needs complete ownership by empowered managers that can build performance through the support of the entire employee population. This demonstrates the full commitment to the discovery process and to the possible change initiatives. Even recognition should be shared for the embracement and implementation of organizational changes.

As already stated, conducting an engagement survey can provide a tremendous number of insights along with the potential identification of targets for focus that can enhance organizational performance.

Here are details on five survey program components.

Component One – *Crafting the employee engagement survey.*

Developing a customized questionnaire should be based on the grouping of about 50 questions. Having to many questions (70 - 80) can be overwhelming for the participants, and having too few items (20 to 30 in number) may not be specific enough. The survey impact can be enhanced with the use of validated benchmarking data that is built into the survey. All of the questions need to be very clear and focused. A 5-point rating scale is the norm. The questions can be grouped into several areas – such as teamwork, work-life balance, customer support, and compensation. Other groupings could be – development & growth opportunities, organizational vision & mission, communication, leadership openness & respect, and diversity. There can even be a few open-ended questions requiring written feedback opinions specific to the organization's strength, as well as areas for improvement.

Here are some examples of closing questions.

➢ Are you passionate about the company?
➢ Do you believe your contributions are important and values?
➢ Do you actively support the corporate strategies?

Based on a well-designed engagement survey and discovery process, a high-engagement culture can be grown over time. Employees connected to their work, recognized for their strengths and abilities to contribute, should lead to enhanced managerial credibility and integrity.

Component Two – *Building an effective process plan and project approach*

Establishing specific timelines and several implementation phases are a part of assembling the rollout activities. All of these pieces are based on values, drivers, and consequences that are connected by well-defined measurements, benchmarks and modeling techniques. There are usually six primary steps in the timeline – preparation, launch, results-review, results-debriefing, communication (both pre-and post), and group meetings specific to ownership and actions. Again, the actual measurements are based on several factors, such as worker enthusiasm, commitment, and connection to organizational goals, as well as employee satisfaction and pride in their work and the company. Other measures could be defined motivators and the willingness to apply discretionary effort. The process plan must have identified builders of engagement such as trust in leadership, personal recognition, commitment to developing skills, and a willingness to work hard and do the best possible job. Key for success with this process is to have a complete connection and commitment by the organization to the defined project plan and approach.

Component Three – *Assembling a communication approach*

Based on the commitment by top leadership to the survey process and the identified organizational benefits, the execution of all of the components of the communication approach is critical in building involvement, trust, and intentions. The employee connections and feedback communications must be aligned at all company levels, and especially, on a global basis. The initial step is establishing an orientation discussion on survey expectations, benefits, and required dedication. Management roles need to be well defined in the process. The second step of the "event" needs to focus on the purpose of the survey, the actual value, and the process that will be utilized. There is an excitement generated regarding the implementation that surfaces based on this unique opportunity of sharing specific input about organizational needs and potential for change. Next, a handle on follow-up activities requires a focus on sharing results, and setting up departmental / management meetings. This is the beginning of the establishment of actions and the addressing of issues going forward. The forth step is providing communication on results in a positive and open fashion. Group discussions and targeted action planning need to focus on the short and long-term goals. The final communication activities need to be on-going and regular to help maintain employee connections to the survey results. Key will be to look at drivers of performance and to recognize specific impact aspects, such as customer service, effective communication, strong executive leadership, innovation, marketing dynamics, and quality improvements.

Component Four – *Gathering and analyzing survey data*

Survey input is the foundation for discoveries along with potential targets for company improvements and enhancements. These responses can actually influence policies and strategies. The targets can be compared to benchmarked data and used to set priorities as well as build programs for change. Demographics will also have an influence on possible opportunities along with alignment of programs with business strategies. Many "learnings" can be a focus for further assessment, such as internally - employee attrition rates, and externally - customer loyalty and satisfaction. Ultimately, the analytical data will be the foundation for significant long-term change and for improving business performance.

Component Five – *Assembling and implementing organizational tactics and action steps*

Based on the survey input and discoveries, careful business strategies and improvement action steps need to be assembled and communicated. Implementing change initiatives must be done with care and be based on collaborative as well as specific follow-through activities. It is important to recognize that some actual findings may have significant and serious consequences. Champions and executive sponsorship will help drive accountability for the impact on performance. All action steps should be well aligned with both the short-term and long-term goals and objectives of the company. And, regular feedback meetings must occur along with the distribution of survey reports that evolve over time.

A successful and well-executed engagement survey can actually drive a competitive advantage for the business, enhance employee retention, and build improved outcomes. Changes can truly occur through the evolution of behaviors with passion and emotions. And, the contributions made by employees utilizing the survey action steps should always be appreciated and recognized publicly.

Personal Story - Business Acumen

Building business knowledge and product application insights can be gained by connecting with internal company product designers and production assemblers, as well as by learning about the actual use and application from product end-users. As part of the leadership team at Datascope Corp., a small medical device company with its headquarters in Montvale, New Jersey, it was important for me to have a positively enthusiastic level of energy and passion for Intra-aortic balloon and pump product lines. This helped enhance the business acumen needed to hire the best candidates for all positions, capable of driving the performance and growth of the company.

One of my critical components of being a human resource leader at Datascope was to find and attract strong individuals for sales, marketing, research & development, finance, as well as for product production positions. Key was to select candidates that could meet the expectations of the specific jobs and handle the challenges within a complex medical device organization. The only way to accomplish this task successfully was to get fully engaged in the business of the Intra-aortic balloon pump (IABP) therapy and to develop an understanding of the important value of this cardiac support device for the actual end users, the patients. So, the solution was to go into the field and visit hospitals, and actually see balloon insertions in the catheterization lab / operating rooms. Also, connecting and talking with doctors and nurses about CABG procedures – coronary artery bypass grafts, helped provide further insights into medical heart repairs and how the Datascope IABP product / therapy impacted patient well-being.

A visit to Resurrection Hospital in the Chicago area was one of my greatest learning and discovery experiences. The hospital connections became the basis for my understanding of the critical nature of receiving cardiac support and repair, a huge influence on patient survival. I witnessed open heart surgery and the performance of a by-pass procedure. Wow! I also spent time in the catheterization lab and observed the insertion of an Intra-aortic balloon that resulted in the improvement of the patient's health. Besides chatting with cardiac surgeons and interventional doctors, I met with nurses and purchasing agents at the hospital. These were the individuals that sales individuals needed to interface with to be able to support hospital and product needs. My exposure to the product users and the hospital environment provided a better understanding of the complexity of the sales and marketing roles, and the importance of identifying candidates that could best handle the challenges within the medical marketplace. Besides product knowledge, there were emotionally demanding aspects associated with these positions.

Beyond the visits to other hospitals, walking the Datascope production floors where intra-aortic balloons are produced and where the very complex IAB pumps are assembled, also provided a deeper product and business knowledge foundation. And, by experiencing the passion these production employees have for their jobs and the products they "build", I personal gained a special perspective on the importance of the Datascope business for the actual heart patient. All of these activities helped me establish the focus of the human resource department specific to growing an organization with employees that have the correct competencies along with the personal desires to perform their jobs with total commitment. Learning and growing is a continuous journey for leaders that requires business acumen and knowledge insights. By building high-performing sales and marketing teams, enhancing a strong R&D function, and supporting dedicated production workers, the company was able to exceed business performance expectations and to drive strong organizational financial successes.

Personal Story - Engagement

Through the understanding of levels of employee motivation and worker engagement, leaders can gain insights into organizational performance and customer satisfaction. So, by learning about influencing factors specific to employee engagement, leaders can better focus their company strategies and long-term vision to enhance successes in many areas. They can impact employee passion for their jobs and the overall emotional commitment to the complete business. Ultimately, building a high-performing workforce can truly influence innovation, creativity, and bottom-line growth. Leaders with strong applicable competencies and leadership skills can drive employee engagement, provide learning and development opportunities for growth, and improve work-life balance for all workers at all levels and positions throughout the organization.

During 2012, the global medical technology organization that I worked for at the time – The Getinge Group, headquarter in Sweden – committed to and conducted a global Employee Engagement Survey with the support of Kenexa/IBM. (The selection process was described in Chapter Three on Critical Thinking.) This complex undertaking connected with about 15,000 employees in over 34 countries. It utilized a very carefully prepared and robust assessment vehicle, focused on measuring employee engagement levels and on building the feedback findings into action-oriented steps. Ultimately, the action steps and enhanced processes that were implemented could impact employee commitment and aid with many organizational changes as well as growth.

The broad purpose of the engagement survey was to use a change movement tool and to gain an understanding of factors that "caused employees to work harder, stay longer, and care more about the organization". The challenge was to measure an individual's involvement and commitment to their work, and to discover the psychological investment employees' were making with the organization.

There were two primary survey targeted outcomes.

1. To identify items that could drive changes and bring about organizational improvements.

2. To secure insights regarding business areas that could be used to build a potential employee brand.

The consulting organization (Kenexa/IBM) was identified and a Getinge Group support team was established along with survey champion leaders. The project occurred over four quarters with care placed on the ability to address specific issues such as the required languages, the actual survey structure, the data collection, and the approach to driving outcome ownership. There were a multiple number of steps taken.

- Having kick-off meetings
- Assembling of a survey draft and questions, and testing content
- Establishing the survey methodology and communication materials
- Building a data administration approach
- Finalizing the reporting structure and general logistics
- Training survey champions and actually launching the survey globally
- Assessing data and building reports
- Holding action step meetings
- Conducting post-project reviews

There were many special requirements that needed to be addressed.

- The number of translations and determination of clarity of the languages
- The use of paper-based survey versus on-line structure and format
- Identification of country survey champions and country ownership
- Assembly of the communication pieces along with a distribution schedule
- The ideal use of the ten specific leadership competencies – action oriented; leading; managing people; building

relationships; analyzing; thinking strategically; planning; managing change; entrepreneurial drive; results orientation

Ultimately, the survey project was focused on sustainable growth through the development of the employee population. Leadership competencies were further driven based on four foundational cornerstones – "inspiring others, taking initiative, driving innovation, and delivering results". Skills, knowledge, and behaviors became the focus for change. Other factors were incorporated into the engagement discovery process, specific to employee and customer loyalty, company brand and image, corporate profits, and development programs based on change management. With lots of time and energy, the survey was well received, and it provided long-term impact for the Getinge Group.

Personal Story - Leadership Styles

Working and experiencing leader relationships has been an outstanding learning discovery process. It is clear that leaders have primary and secondary leadership styles impacting their management of organizational strategies and mission. Leadership is an art, a science, and a craft based on *human chemistry*. The learning insights and newly gained understandings that are described below were the result of connecting and working with many leaders at all levels. Key was to recognize that leaders have personal styles based on several different aspects - their imagination, creativity, innovation, visioning, mentorship, and communication. They have different levels of passion for excellence, various levels of fear associated with challenges, and varying expectations of themselves as well as for the workforce.

Without identifying the actual leader, here are five examples of different leadership styles, along with the lessons learned as part of my leadership journey. There are no right or wrong styles, just one that is utilized by that specific leader.

Leader "W" worked for a European based manufacturing company. Although on the younger side, this leader was a very confident and competent individual. He operated out of the corporate headquarters, and oversaw a global employee population. His leadership style was a combination of conservatively fun innovativeness and democratic commitment to the organization.

> Working with this leader provided a learning experience based on his style of freedom to create and drive engaging employee projects and activities. Complete trust, support and acceptance of ideas and input resulted in many great outcomes. A very comprehensive talent management portfolio was developed and distributed to all managers. A challenging and exciting executive development program was built and launched. Clearly, great supportive behaviors, perfect direction, and strong encouragement led to outstanding successes for the organization.

Leader "V" was a division president and CEO of a global manufacturing organization. This leader was an individual from Germany, taking on a key role in the US business. He was extremely authoritarian, very controlling, and overly structured. Even though highly focused on the business, he was also focused on himself, and unfortunately, less on the employee population. He lacked the understanding of the importance of humility. He remained very task focused and overly command and control oriented.

> Working with this leader provided insights into the importance of collaboration as well as having personal self-awareness of the value of humility and authenticity. Being a leader requires a true connection to the long-term vision and the future. Yet, taming personal tenacity and persistence needs to occur so one can jump hurdles and obstacles to drive

strong business outcomes, along with maintaining positive and engaging attitudes.

Leader "Y" was a past leader within the medical diagnostic world and focused on driving production at a manufacturing organization of complex therapeutic products. Although somewhat technical in nature, this leader was very relationship oriented and a strong driver of a collaborative vision built on clear core values. He recognized the impact and importance of open communication with the employee population at all levels. He was big on regular connecting meetings, both large and small, as well as on Town Hall meetings that were very engaging. There were events to celebrate successes. This leader was a dynamic persuasive-influencer and a great driver of change along with growth.

> Working with this leader demonstrated the importance and impact of connecting with colleagues as well as all employees. Walking-and-talking really can make a difference in building engagement and commitment. Leaders and top executives that show a caring attitude along with a sense of humor can truly enhance overall people and organizational effectiveness.

Leader "X" was a human resource officer of a US based company with global service and product distribution. This leader was a trust builder with a strong willingness to empower direct reports as well as to encourage creative thinking. He was very relationship oriented and a creator of team harmony. Besides having clear policies and procedures, this leader was extremely supportive of a learning and growth-driven culture.

> Working with this leader opened the door to the building of a coaching culture along with an effective approach to

personally developing stronger leadership competencies. A learning process and a caring-leader approach helped drive more emotional engagement as well as a commitment to the organization. Self-aware and skilled coaching leaders and managers at all levels learn to take calculated risks and enhance their comfort with ambiguity and conflict.

Leader "Z" was a highly seasoned and experienced business leader, providing direction and services within the medical device manufacturing world. This intelligent leader was highly structured with organizational strategies and direction. He expected and demanded the highest level of problem-solving based on explicit details and personal insights. As a pacesetter, he was very action and results driven.

Working with this leader enhanced the importance of using a more powerful approach to communicating company needs and articulating organizational challenges and expectations. For example, by providing only a few solutions to a problem always resulted in a request for additional insights and methods. So, a process based on carefully reviewing many concerns and presenting several approaches to specific obstacles became the critical success factor for the best outcomes. Long-term goals were always a key component to every review discussion.

Closing Remarks

Companies are constantly evolving – such as consolidating management structures and acquiring new business, redesigning the workforce and reorganizing the employee base, and transitioning leaders into new positions and restructuring the leadership teams. Leaders need to evolve and grow throughout their leadership business life and fully understanding their actual roles and demands. They must build insights about personal capabilities, and continuously enhance their competencies as well as marketplace knowledge. There are many components associated with the development of current and future leaders. And, based on *human chemistry*, closing leadership skill gaps can clearly impact the bottom-line and profit successes of an organization.

Leaders need to grow throughout their careers and their leadership learning journeys. They need to master the art of self-awareness, to cultivate relationships, and to build an inspiring culture.

- Leaders help maintain perspective and enhance levels of clarity within team relationships.
- Leaders build a strong focus on people and always take time to actively listen with passion.
- Leaders utilize both their tangible competencies (the hard skills) and their intangible traits (the soft skills).
- Leaders have compassion, openness, empathy and generosity, and are always looking for the good in others.
- Leaders find what inspires others and ignite their engagement in their jobs as well as the organization.
- Leaders embrace all actions along with being accountable for their decisions and plans.

Leaders need personal self-awareness and an understanding on what they want from their people, along with a strong handle on what people need and desire from their leaders.

Leadership is about *human chemistry*
    – the connection of leaders to PEOPLE and to their HEARTS.

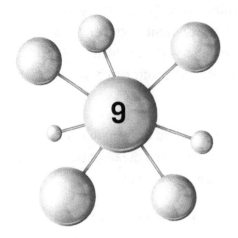

LEADERSHIP AND WISDOM

Leaders committed to people and human chemistry.

The Chemistry Connection

Our world continues to evolve rapidly based on technology requirements and needs associated with the advancements of solar energy, communication devices, and batteries for electric cars. This has
caused a higher demand for specialty minerals made up of complex
structures of elements, such as oxygen, silicon, aluminum, iron, cal-
cium, potassium and magnesium. These seven elements account
for about 98% of the earth's crust. And, other elements are also
used in technology manufacturing, such as indium, tellurium, gal-
lium, lithium and cobalt.

Higher levels of diversity and enhanced competencies in leadership
are becoming more critical for new ways to deal with the fast evolving organizations and challenging work environments. Company
structures and business approaches continue to become more

complex, requiring new resources and capabilities. Leaders need to possess stronger abilities to inspire and motivate others, to effectively drive results, and to focus on getting things done more quickly. Similar to the elements and minerals that are a critical component in building valued products of the future, leadership needs to be more focused on authentic realism and on passionate achievement orientation. Leaders need to have diverse levels of competencies and capabilities to drive a clear as well as engaging vision and direction for growing organizations.

Future leaders need to be driven by personal accountability for the ultimate **G-O-A-L** mindset based on trust and integrity.

- G – **Genuine** recognition provider
- O – **Open** communication connector
- A – **Authentic** relationship builder
- L – **Leader** presence enhancer

Leadership with a Personal Commitment to People

Leaders building human partnerships and relationships.

We are living in a fast-changing and constantly evolving world. There are higher levels of uncertainty as well as complexity, and change has become the constant.

- ➤ The social network, Facebook, has over two billion monthly users globally.
- ➤ Prescription drugs, Opioids, have become an increasingly addiction problem.
- ➤ Renewable energy has surpassed nuclear power generation.
- ➤ Climate change has caused the ocean waters to rise.
- ➤ Government is challenged by the need for leadership authenticity and trust.

Leadership is more than just a science, more than just an art, and more than just a craft. Leadership is founded on *human chemistry* – the ability for a leader to look inward and to become fully self-aware, and the ability for a leader to look outward and to build an understanding of others. Specifically, leaders need to meet the needs of people – employees, managers, directors, colleagues, teams, shareholders, and even external customers and personal connections. Therefore, the focus of a leader is not on themselves, but on others. Leaders need to communicate openly, listen more, be honest with the facts, have an inspiring vision, and be accountable for their actions. Leaders also need to be compassionate and empathetic, and to be able to use both emotional and social intelligence to build relationships.

Every leader has their own personal "chemistry" associated with their behaviors, thinking dynamics, managerial actions, performance approaches, and ways of connecting with people. As much as employees work to meet the needs of leaders and the company, leaders must also meet the needs of their employee base.

There are six components specific to building strong human partnerships and bonds between leaders and the organizational population.

One – Connections and Direction

What does the employee population need from their leaders?

They want leaders to provide clarity of direction and expectations, helping to translate goals into actions as well as deliverables. In a motivating and supportive fashion, both the short-term goals and the long-term vision need to be carefully articulated through open communications. The goals need to be realistic and reasonable, yet have some amount of stretch. The vision message needs to be dynamic and compelling. Leaders need to share the company strategies authentically and to get others to believe in the vision by focusing on the future. They provide the purpose for the organization and for each individual's role. With an optimistic "line-of-sight", the leader helps everyone embrace change and add value to an evolving business as well as to the bottom-line.

Two – Empowerment and Ownership

What does the employee population need from their leaders?

They want leaders to embrace their strategic responsibilities and to be fully accountable for their actions. With high levels of passion and enthusiasm for their leadership roles, leaders must help others address business challenges and impact organizational changes. Based on complete and proactive ownership of their positions, leaders can build employee loyalty and commitment to job achievement as well as to the delivery on goal expectations. Leaders, also, need to empower employees to be involved in the building of global plans and strategies, along with the desired metrics. Leaders need to manage, coach, and support the employee population so that each individual can successfully execute the vision and jump obstacles when they surface.

Three – Recognition and Appreciation

What does the employee population need from their leaders?

They want leaders to utilize the power of caring, showing true emotions and feelings. Leaders must demonstrate gratitude and acknowledge achievements and contributions to the organization. Through praise and positive kindness, a leader encourages loyalty and commitment to the company. And, by building employee engagement and satisfaction, a leader drives higher levels of retention. Key is for leaders to encourage employees to use their strengths, to regularly review performance at all levels, and to celebrate individual as well as organizational successes.

Four – Innovative Culture and Environment

What does the employee population need from their leaders?

They want leaders to always value creativity and innovation by others. This can be achieved by driving a culture of learning and an environment of development. Many diverse learning processes can be followed – such as the encouragement of the sharing of knowledge and information, formal development programs, on-line courses, and on-the-job experiences. Leaders need to accept some levels of failure by others and even demonstrate their own vulnerability by indicating that trying new things is okay. Leaders need to help others find joy through self-discovery and build a culture based on win-win solutions. Leaders must support the growth of people and the development of talent for the future.

Five – High Levels of Honesty and Transparency

What does the employee population need from their leaders?

They want leaders to be open and authentic with their behaviors and with their communication activities. Consistency, honesty, and integrity are the foundational components to being a trusted leader. These leadership values are further impacted by having humility and by sharing true personal feelings. Through their compassion and empathy, leaders build their credibility and respect, and motivate positive behaviors in others.

Six – Relationship and Partnerships

What does the employee population need from their leaders?

They want leaders to constantly drive cross-functional and cross-organizational relationships. Through collaborative partnerships and teams, leaders can demonstrate their pride and confidence in others. Their leadership effectiveness is enhanced through agile and adaptive behaviors. Leaders need to listen more, talk less, tune-in and make discoveries. Supportive and helpful behaviors along with no preconceived judgements, can result in the growth of partnerships and in the building of employee commitment to the organization.

People Perspective

Based on the *human chemistry* specific to leadership, leaders must recognize that people are all different. They have different needs and different expectations. They are influenced by the organizational culture, previous employment and choices made in the past. Therefore, leaders need to recognize that creative and unusual approaches to engagement will be required to positive influence a variety of people-types that have a diversity of mindsets.

To gain perspective, people can be grouped or categorized based on behavioral characteristics, thinking styles, communication approaches, and learning requirements. The following structure is an extremely generalized approach, yet it can provide insights for leaders about people, and help with making discoveries into meeting the specific needs of others. There can be three or four or even eight to twelve people groups. Yet, I have established five groups specific to people traits.

1. Structured People Traits

2. Analytical People Traits

3. Expressive People Traits

4. Reflective People Traits

5. Creative People Traits

Before providing the details on each of these people groups, it is important to recognize that leaders can gain additional insights through the use of assessment instruments and diagnostic tools. There are many well-established evaluation "systems" or documents that can provide understanding into an individual's thinking style, social communications, and managerial approaches. A few examples are as follows:

- The Myers-Briggs Type Indicator (MBTI) based on 16 personality types (1)

- The FIRO-B instrument – Fundamental Interpersonal Relations Orientation-Behavior (2)

- Human Synergistics specific to thinking styles (3)

- Blake and Mouton's Management Grid (4)

- Hertzberg's model on motivation (5)

- DDI-Development Dimensions International (6)

- OPQ32 (7)

- DISC personality types (8)

- TDF International – T-Lens / D-Lens / F-Lens (9)

- The IOL Tool – Individual / Oriented / Leadership (10)

All of these instruments and tools can help build awareness of personality styles, insights into individual strengths and weaknesses, along with the identification of differences in people. Leader self-awareness can serve as the foundation for their personal behavioral approaches to connecting with others. And, it is important for a leader to understand the environment in which each individual exists, and to utilize their influence to impact the success or failure of the individual in their work and life.

Structured People

These individuals are somewhat rigid in make-up and may even seem potentially narrow-minded as thinkers. They are masters of tasks and defined activities. They can be strong contributors to an organization based on their attention to the details and disciplined approaches to job expectations. They assemble complex plans, review each step with care, execute with caution, and assess outcomes with a defined structure. They clearly follow their lists step-by-step. They can drive decision-making with consistency and within the established rules, yet can seem to be a little stiff in nature as well as judgmental in their behaviors.

Analytical People

These individuals are complex thinkers and also follow the rules as well as established standards, similar to Structured People. Yet, they may be more perfectionistic in nature, building outcomes on accuracy and quality. Besides being well organized, they evaluate and analyze the details and facts based on logic before taking actions. As data-based problem solvers, they are conservative risk-takers. Even though less assertive than others, and somewhat quiet at times, these individuals have high levels of perseverance. They carefully use their resources so that they can create positive organizational impact and outcomes.

Expressive People

These individuals are enthusiastic and high energy-oriented people connectors. Their extroverted and outgoing behaviors can even make the expressive person to be pereived as an outspoken "talker" at times and seen as a performer. Their assertive approaches to situations demonstrates social confidence and high levels of optimism with their relationships. The aspects of emotions and feelings contain compassion and a supportive nature. Their adaptive dynamics are reinforced through recognition and praise. These individuals are fun-loving, joyful, and even flamboyant with their sense of humor. Yet, they are always respectful of others.

Reflective People

These individuals are very thoughtful, fair and considerate in nature, and seen as amiable types. As team players and even dreamers at times, they are able to build strong relationships. They have a cooperative approach to their roles, slow-paced and reserved, yet may avoid conflict at times. These individuals take their position responsibilities very seriously and always follow ethical paths with humility. Key for their success is based on the ability to seek depth of understanding in all situations.

Creative People

These individuals are imaginative thinkers, innovative and out-of-the-box drivers of performance and valued contributions. Their spontaneous and open-ended approaches can help achieve unexpected solutions to problems, even ones that may be viewed as superficial. By being less organized at times, these independent minded individuals can help build and encourage higher levels of exploration.

As stated earlier, leaders need to focus on people, employees, and teams, to help drive the successful performance of an organization.

The Frances Hesselbein Leadership Institute drives "impact" by fostering leadership grounded in "the passion to serve" "the discipline to listen" "the courage to question" "and the spirit to include". (11)

As detailed throughout this book, Leadership is about **human chemistry** – the connection of leaders to <u>PEOPLE</u> and to their <u>HEARTS</u>.

P – People partnerships and passion for presence
E – Engagement and execution
O – Openness through transparency
P – Purpose and a compelling plan
L – Loyalty through leadership
E – Energy and enthusiasm

H – Honesty and humility
E – Empathy and ethical behaviors
A – Authenticity and acknowledgement of achievement
R – Realistic relationships and recognition
T – Trust and teamwork
S – Sincerity and spirit of compassion

Finding Wisdom throughout the Leadership Learning Journey

A growth process based on self-reflection and self-discovery.

We are living and growing in a very complex world with a high level of unpredictability and vulnerability.

As per Marcel Proust (a French novelist who lived from 1871 to 1922), "The real voyage of discovery consists not in seeing new landscapes, but in having new eyes." (12)

Life is a learning journey. And, wisdom is one of the greatest outcome achievements specific to having exceptional experiences, engaging relationships, and fantastic discoveries along the daily pathway. Leadership capabilities and competencies grow through the utilization and the application of the various learnings. The key realization is that leaders have a diversity of leadership styles, skills, and behaviors. Personal and insightful wisdom and self-awareness by leaders are used to build successful business accomplishments through the valued influence on the organizational working population.

The Reflections and the Directions

Leadership is about using the head and the heart. It is about motivating employees and gaining their commitment to drive business performance along with the ability to address the accelerated pace of change. Wise leaders are on a pathway of constant growth, evolving and developing creative thinking capabilities and competencies throughout their journey. They have learned to develop their abilities to engage, and not to control others. They have focused on gaining regular and constructive feedback, and on having a passion to enhance corporate successes and outcomes. Greater self-awareness and a willingness to take risks helps achieve outstanding results. Leadership wisdom clearly impacts the ability of a leader to add value to the organization and to bring harmony with society.

The Journey and the Learnings

Effective leadership is about driving strategies and actions into strong business results, and gaining positive outcomes based on a focus specific to reality and values. To be a flexible and engaging leader, and to be able to meet the demands of the evolving business situations, many different leadership competencies must be utilized. They are the abilities and experiences such as developing personal self-awareness, having the desire to motivate others, discovering inner empathy, and finding the importance of social skills to influence others. All of these capabilities have grown throughout life based on the many business experiences and people interactions of the leader. This has helped define the outstanding wisdom gained throughout the leadership learning journey.

Wise leaders have developed an exceptional handle on managing challenges and on utilizing judgement in driving difficult decisions. And, it has been achieved with a focus on authenticity and openness. They have found ways to know people well, to read them with high levels of accuracy, and to be able to gather many details for the greatest depth of understanding. Leadership competencies have been grown to strategically drive an inspire vision along with a common sense of direction for the future of an organization. Strong, clear, and potentially vulnerable communication is necessary to enhance results. A well-focused and confident leader can clearly provide a company with a competitive advantage in the marketplace. Therefore, discoveries become part of the personal wisdom of a leader and the foundation for their long-term goals. This leadership wisdom is formulated through a combination of values, intelligence, and judgement. The learning journey of the leader contains passion, risk-taking, and willingness to share joy.

The Discoveries and the Outcomes

As already stated, leadership wisdom has grown from challenging experiences, enhanced expertise, and developed knowledge. This wisdom has built an impact on judgements, decisions-making, and action implementation. The specific focus on the future of an organization is based on a clear company purpose and mission, on benefits to society, and the ability to build economic value. Leaders with wisdom have learned to actively listen, to build engaging relationships and partnerships, and to communicate with high levels of authenticity and clarity. They have discovered the true value of face-to-face conversations and powerful connections, resulting in the ability to drive successful business actions into organizational accomplishments – all through the outstanding *human chemistry* of the leader.

A Personal Closing Story – Talent Management

Leaders create value and tackle many challenges. They focus on organizational changes and the employee mindset, attitudes, perceptions and feelings. Leaders drive the ROI and take accountability for talent acquisition, performance management, employee engagement, and for driving a culture of change. Without a doubt, long-term sustainability is founded on strong company performance, innovative business approaches, and a dynamic culture.

I became a global team member and organizational partner with a group of five human resource leaders and three divisional business executive heads, all connected to the human resource corporate leader. The worldwide company, the Getinge Group, had its headquarters located in Sweden. The goal of this team of eight, under the direction of the corporate leader, was to custom-craft a talent management portfolio that would be used by all business units throughout the 34 global locations. Ultimately, this carefully built document would be the foundation to help drive major corporate changes as well as deliver critically important business results. The portfolio needed to inspire leaders, managers, and employees to enthusiastically and energetically drive their personal performance behaviors and competencies. Leaders at all levels of the evolving organization needed to take full ownership and to proactively enhance solutions specific to the business challenges. They needed to enhance the passion for the long-term goals and the big picture of the organization for the future.

This unique and extremely dedicated global team was committed and charged to build a talent management portfolio that focused on leadership effectiveness along with the encouragement of an openness for new perspectives and exceptional thinking mindsets. The portfolio was to serve as the foundation for *human chemistry* management and leadership.

- To drive the ability to communicate, negotiate and lead successfully.
- To drive the ability to enhance interpersonal skills and trust along with respect.
- To drive the ability to achieve outstanding performance results.
- To drive the ability to build high levels of self-confidence and empathy.

The ultimate team goal was to craft a corporate portfolio that could support leaders to cultivate and develop the employee population based on their effective action-orientation and emotional leadership norms. The *"Talent Management Portfolio – Sustainable Growth through People Development"* (13) was assembled with six primary components. It also contained the corporate leadership competencies and a talent management calendar.

> *The system was based on four behavioral cornerstones, eight leadership competencies, and four core values that served as the foundation for the evolving leadership culture. Every business action was focused on identifying, assessing, and developing employee talent. The business strategy was to have all performance contributions flow into business results through employee engagement and personal growth. (14)*

All six components of the portfolio were structured based on several key pieces. Each component contained a description of the philosophy for each process, an overview as well as guidelines, and some details on the "who, what, how, and when".

Here is a picture of the Talent Management Portfolio content.

Section One: **Performance Management & Development Process -** Tools and techniques to build effective performance.

> As per Steve Garvey, *"You have to set goals that are almost out of reach. If you set a goal that is attainable without much work or thought, you are stuck with something below your true talent and potential."* (15)

Performance management is a partnership between the manager and employee that supports the growth and effectiveness of employees. It is a process which builds on individual competencies, skills and knowledge, and aligns their goals with the strategies of the organization. By having a clear performance process, managers and employees can help drive the goal setting, execution and assessment activities. Through regular interactive communication and coaching, employees can grow and develop within the organization.

Performance review discussions help add focus and direction with regards to position expectations. As employees grow and develop, their levels of engagement and retention continue to increase, which positively impacts business outcomes.

Performance is defined as a review of "what" has been accomplished, balanced with "how" the results were achieved. Performance discussions need to occur on a regular and ongoing basis with a minimum of one informal and engaging discussion each quarter. Performance reviews can serve as an important tool for motivation, attitude and behavior development, as well as for communicating and aligning individual and organizational aims that foster positive relationships between managers and their direct reports. Based on careful preparation, an effective performance management process enables managers to evaluate and measures individual performance and optimize productivity. Review discussions can help tighten the link between strategic business objectives and day-to-day actions. The performance practices all can positively impact employee retention and loyalty.

Effective goal setting with clear timelines, combined with a method to track progress and identify obstacles, contributes to possible performance successes. Regular tracking of progress against defined goals and objectives provides opportunity to recognize and reward employees. Development plans are critical outcomes that keep driving employee growth and learning, and open doors to meet career aspirations and to moving into future positions.

Section Two: **Succession Planning Process** - A talent management process strategically focused on sustaining organizational health and ensuring business growth.

As per Peter F. Drucker, *"Management is doing things right; leadership is doing the right things."* (16)

Succession planning is a process for identifying, assessing and developing talented employees so that they are able to fill critical positions and to help meet the needs of the organization now and in the future. This proactive planning approach is focused on getting the rights successors with the right skills into key positions. The process utilizes internal individuals in a cost effective and a career oriented way. This strategic talent management process ensures that the organization can achieve its business objectives and retain competitive knowledge as well as competencies.

There are many business benefits to utilizing the succession planning process. Besides retaining individuals with key skills and knowledge, internal promotions are far more cost effective than external talent acquisition. It creates career paths for employees as well as provides development opportunities that are motivating and future focused. There is a time-saving aspect to filling positions internally, and aligns the right people with the strategic organizational objectives. And, finally, it prepares the organization to deal with sudden, catastrophic losses of key people.

There are several steps and components that help drive a successful succession activity. All key and strategic positions for the long-term health of the organization and for business success need to be identified. These roles are identified as areas requiring strong contributions and vital tasks at all levels. One must also identify potential successors that can be considered likely candidates, able to assume new positions within one to five years. Several assessment methods can be followed, and assembled into data documents. Vacancy risks and successor readiness need be evaluated specific to timing. Special competencies for development can be included along with geographic mobility and language skills. Talent review meetings need to occur regularly so that a succession pipeline of talent can be assembled.

Action plans should involve additional testing, behavioral interviews, and work simulations. Finally, strategic direction must be set by senior management and human resource leadership regarding the needed growth and development of the identified individuals.

<u>Section Three:</u> **High Potential Talent Identification Process** - Evaluate high potential talent employees and drive their development.

As per Maya Angelou, *"I've learned that people will forget what you say, people will forget what you did, but people will never forget how you made them feel."* (17)

High potential employees consistently and significantly out perform their peer groups in a variety of settings and circumstances. While achieving these superior levels of performance, these elite individuals exhibit behaviors that reflect the organizational culture and values in an exemplary manner. The high potential employee should have a strong capacity to grow and succeed throughout their careers, probably even more quickly and effectively than their peers.

High potentials (sometimes referred to as HiPo) always deliver strong results on a regular basis, master new types of expertise quickly, and personally recognize that behavior counts. It is the intangible factors that truly distinguishes these individuals. They have exceptional drive to excelalong with an enterprising spirit. They have a catalytic learning capacity and a dynamicsensory to read situations and opportunities. These high potential individuals can be at all levels of the organization, and have strong desires to learn and grow. They can be viewed as individuals that will yield the highest return-on-investment for the company. The nine box performance/

potential grid can be used in a confidential way to conduct assessments. Key is to ensure that high potentials are not confused with high performers, that the identified hi-pos are fully engaged, and that development occurs at a variety of levels.

Section Four: **Learning & Development Process** - Combining experience, relationships and education to enable personal growth and preparations for future challenges.

As per The Gallup Organization, *"Individuals who feel that their own development is being encouraged, and who have had opportunities to learn and grow, tend to have stronger engagement and performance."* (18)

Learning is a process of providing avenues for growth and development – basically, unlocking the mind, uncovering strengths, and enhancing relationships and leadership competencies. Key is to build talent that is aligned with business objectives and accountable for individual achievements. Employees develop their career paths based on a framework of learning. There are many ways to structure L&D activities, and the approaches are changing at an accelerated pace. Besides all forms of online learning, formal-classroom training remains an important part of the development process. On-the-job experiences, stretch assignments, teamwork, networking, and even feedback processes are all part of growing employees. Coaching, mentoring, and shadowing have taken on more critical roles in L&D.

Workplace learning is critical for developing talent and closing skill gaps for the future. These capabilities can be both hard and soft skills, such as communication abilities, leadership competencies, problem-solving, and collaboration. There are many challenges that need to be addressed regarding making content relevant, handling time constraints, and the multi-generational workforce. And, management must be fully involved in encouraging the L&D cultural mindset to be aligned with company vision and long-term goals.

<u>Section Five:</u> **Rewards and Recognition Process** - Motivating, engaging and building employee loyalty.

As per Aristotle, *"In the arena of human life the honors and rewards fall to those who show their good qualities in action."* (19)

Rewards and recognition are components used to drive employee engagement and commitment to impact organizational achievements and results. The actual approach is based on business as well as human resource strategies, along with the organizational culture. It is built on attracting, motivating and retaining employees in order to support a successful and long-term business direction. The key is to follow a framework that can guide the designand decision-making of the compensation elements specific to base pay, incentive pay, retirement plans, healthcare benefits and other benefits. The reward and recognition process must also look at work-life balance, development, and career growth opportunities.

The compensation strategy focuses on making sure that employees are rewarded fairly and in a timely manner. The three primary components are built on the business and cultural context – attracting and retaining talent, balancing compensation with financial expectations, and always incentivizing as well as rewarding employee contributions. Base pay recognizes the main position responsibilities and is linked to the respective market conditions of the position level as well as the performance of the position holder. Variable pay is non-guaranteed compensation and can come in two forms specific to the position – Sales Incentive Plans and Bonus Plans. Salary reviews occur on an annual basis following an individual performance review. Many principles are applied, such as an individual's performance and present ompensation level. Budgets are drivers along with the actual business areas and the country. All salary changes require compliance audits and proper approvals. And all laws, union agreement and local customs in each country must be followed.

Section Six: **Talent Acquisition Process** - Effective and efficient practices to identify and add top talent to the business.

> As per Larry Bossidy, *"I am convinced that nothing we do is more important than hiring and developing people. At the end of the day you bet on people, not on strategies."* (20)

Philosophically, making great people decisions will undoubtedly help drive organizational performance, as well as enhance chances of personal career success. Finding and attracting talent, interviewing for best position fit, and onboarding great candidates are all challenging experiences. The key is to understand the business needs, learn about the success factors for a position, and gain insights into the skills, competencies and knowledge of each potential new hire. The right talent will join, stay and perform in an evolving and growing organization.

There are several key steps in the talent acquisition/re-cruiting process. Always have a comprehensive position description along with a competency profile. Have the job requisition documentation with the necessary approvals, and proceed to look at internal talent before jumping to the outside. Review resumes/CVs, interview candidates, share assessments, and make the selection. Diversity sourcing is critical in the building and maintaining a diverse workforce. Leaders and hiring managers need to re-vision everything that is done to leverage workforce diversity, and to create value which capitalizes on difference. Keep the acquisition process flowing via the on-boarding, future development activities, enhanced engagement, and regular assessment along with valued feedback. Build on the organizational culture and work environment as a way of introducing new and exciting challenges for the added talent, as well as driving improvement of retention.

A creative and comprehensive performance management portfolio can help leaders address organizational challenges and drive company successes. Leaders and managers of people need to connect with the employee population, establish partnerships, and build relationships. They need to lead and enhance successful performance activities through both formal and informal conversations and feedback sessions. Leaders need to be personally committed to people, self-aware of their roles and their impact on people, and utilize leadership wisdom to drive organizational outcomes. Leadership is a learning journey based on *human chemistry*.

Leadership Wisdom

The Chemistry of LEADERSHIP is about people and human wisdom. Leadership will continue to evolve and transform into a dynamic and adaptive craft based on innovative managerial approaches.

Leaders will continue to build higher levels of self-awareness throughout their leadership learning journey. They will use three personal components.

❖ The Heart – embracing their roles with emotion and listening with feelings.
❖ The Mind – communicating with inspiration and influencing with confidence.
❖ The Body – connecting with energy and driving actions with reality.

There are many success factors that current and future leaders will use to be effective at meeting many challenges and building strong business outcomes. They will use their competencies to make decisions, to take risks, and to finding courage. Here are five areas that can amplify your leadership self-awareness thoughts and to open your door to be a transformational leader.

One – The a*bility to build authentic trust and loyalty.*

The transformational leader needs to be open, honest and respectful, and clearly, not ever operating egotistically. The leader needs to accept the fact that there is always a cause and an effect. There is a need for an unprecedented level of transparency and visibility in a culture of loyalty. Professionalism becomes the norm in the alignment of actions with words, demonstrating a focus of caring about people. A diversity of followers is truly empowered and dedicated to the consequences of their actions. Authentic trust and complete loyalty is based on the integrity of a leader and their ability to turn promises into reality.

As per Stephen Covey in his book *The Speed of Trust*, "There is one thing that is common to every individual, relationship, team, family, organization, nation, economy, and civilization throughout the world – one thing which, if removed, will destroy the most powerful government, the most successful business, the most thriving economy, the most influential leadership, the greatest friendship, the strongest character, the deepest love. On the other hand, if developed and leveraged, that one thing has the potential to create unparalleled success and prosperity in every dimension of life. That one thing is trust." (21)

Two – The ability to clearly communicate and to enhance connective relationships.

The transformational leader needs to show commitment and enthusiasm in all communications as well as negotiation. They must have truthful, open, and credible connections with the employee population that is built on factual accuracy. There is more asking and listening versus telling, and especially, there is no blaming or twitter wars. There is a move from "I" to "we". Relationships are built on collaboration and accountability, adapting to priorities with an honest commitment to results. This transformational leader clearly and effectively demonstrates self-confidence and empathy along with strong interpersonal and social skills.

> As per Max de Pree in his book *Leadership is an Art*, "In most vital organizations, there is a common bond of interdependence, mutual interest, interlocking contributions, and simple joy. Part of the art of leadership is to see that this common bond is maintained and strengthened, a task certainly requiring good communication. Just as any relationship requires honest and open communication to stay healthy, so the relationships within corporations improve when information is shared accurately and freely." (22)

Three- The ability to drive a dynamic and integrated strategic long-term vision.

The transformational leader needs to consistently create, establish, and communicate a compelling and engaging strategic long-term vision. There is a need to assemble a foundation for a futuristic thinking and a forward driving approach to shape a challenging purpose for the organization. The leader builds an engaging culture, balancing short-term impact goals with realistic long-term objectives. Detailed vision clarity must be enthusiastically moved forward with optimism. A consistent leadership message needs to encourage a strong willingness to step out of comfort zones and to utilize positive values as well as behaviors.

> As per Eric Mosley and Derek Irvine in their book *The Power of Thanks,* "Great leaders set a purpose and vision for a company by the goals they establish, the values they promote, and the destination they describe. Then they empower the organization to build culture itself, guided by their vision. They hire people who will promote and demonstrate the right cultural values. They build and promote a social architecture that supports the culture they want." (23)

Four – The ability to create an exciting and satisfying work environment.

The transformational leader needs to focus both on growing the business as well as on developing the people. They need to appreciate innovative thinking, dedicated work behaviors, and a strong commitment to the organization. They need to encourage complete involvement in challenging decisions and in finding enjoyment within the work environment. Leaders can drive job experiences so that they become significantly more meaningful, resulting in the enhancement of performance levels to be more efficient and effective.

A supportive learning and development culture accelerates the growth of employee talent, creating individuals that are more successful in addressing challenges as well as opportunities. And, leaders must show on a regular basis higher level of appreciation and acknowledgement of contributions to the organization.

> As per Judith Umlas in her book *Great Leadership,* "Acknowledging your people is a sure way of building genuine trust and a culture of appreciation that can help people give their best efforts. The feelings of appreciation motivate employees to reach out in areas in which they may not feel completely secure but in which they can trust that they can and will be supported." (24)

Five – The ability to establish personal leadership presence and to use nonverbal behaviors

The transformational leader needs to be positively present with employee population and to be active listeners. The leader must be enthusiastic in their leadership approach and attempt to reduce anxieties that could come from being overly controlling and commanding. Their credibility is based on flexibility as well as personal energy. The dedicated and involved leader goes beyond just engagement. They inspire higher levels of commitment and dedication, embrace values and beliefs, and drive elements of sustainability.

> As per Amy Cuddy in her book *PRESENCE – Bringing your Boldest Self to your Biggest Challenges* – "Presence is the state of being attuned to and able to comfortably express our true thoughts, feeling, values, and potential. People who have a solid sense of self-worth reflect that feeling through healthy, effective ways of dealing with challenges and relationships, making them both resilient and more open. Presence manifests as confidence without arrogance." (25)

Closing Thoughts

A Simple Analogy

The challenges within the leadership learning journey can be compared to an airplane trip. The destination is very clearly defined along with the purpose and a focused arrival point. Everyone is working in concert based on trust and respect. Besides the passengers, this includes the pilots, the crew, and ground support. There is complete commitment and a willingness by everyone to conduct their individual responsibilities with collaboration and connections. When difficult weather surfaces, there are quick decisions that are made, adapting to special needs along with being value-oriented. All issues are communicated openly and truthfully, always staying on message – "doing" what is being "said". There is a dynamic and real relationship and partnership between all individuals involved in this journey.

Without a doubt, it is imperative to accept the fact that leaders are operating in a time of turbulence. Leaders need to use competency strengths to energize others. They need to learn to align all leadership components to drive growth, profitability, engagement, commitment, and satisfaction. It is an opportunity to embrace change and fully engage in leadership transformations that encourage curiosity and enthusiasm for a progressive future. Leaders need to balance open humility and assertive energy so that it can ignite innovative curiosity along with long-term commitments. Leaders need to learn to navigate tensions in business during times of uncertainty and transition. Clearly, actions need to result in outcomes that are beyond the status quo. Leaders need courage to look at all business challenges with a willingness to be vulnerable as well as to take responsibility for risk. Manage and lead the present with a vision for shaping the future.

Authentic leaders drive successes through passion and collaboration.

To be successful and effective in a leadership position, the leader must always focus on people and on connecting with others, and clearly, not on themselves. Every day, leaders face many challenges, and they need to be committed to moving organizational projects and business actions forward so that the established goals and inspirational vision can be achieved. Leaders need to have strong relationships, along with personal credibility to influence company outcomes. Dedicated to meeting deadlines and being responsible for essential action-oriented targets are two critical components of the leadership learning journey. They demonstrate the importance of achieving successful and impactful performance. All leadership steps and decisions have aspects of risk and require well-defined and specific, desirable results. Leaders must continuously build their value and trust by demonstrating full involvement and complete ownership in the company strategies.

Teamwork, collaboration, connections throughout an organization, can help enhance employee contributions based on the clarity of direction and a focus on the desired objectives, allowing people to act independently and take personal initiatives. Through higher levels of confidence, leaders as well as their colleagues can move beyond fears, and actually tackle challenges and difficult situations. Team members and individual employees can develop comfort by being accountable for their actions, build strategic mindset, and drive outstanding results. And, leaders must always show appreciation for all contributions as well as acknowledge successes.

There are "twenty" key leadership drivers for effectiveness.

> ➤ Leaders need to **inspire** a pursuit of a common vision
>   ...... never be pessimistic and short-sided.

- Leaders need to constantly focus on their **authenticity** and **credibility**

  ...... never be crazy or unpredictable.

- Leaders need to be **open** and **honest** in their behaviors.

  ...... never ignore established policies and aspects of governance.

- Leaders need to have **morale authority**

  ...... never be ill-equipped to be a leader with total aptitude.

- Leaders need to be **mentally and emotionally stable**

  ...... never be self-centered and disconnected from reality.

- Leaders need to be centered on **collaboration** and **team-work**

  ...... never be a supporter of hazardous or violent solutions.

- Leaders need to be **real** and **down-to-earth**

  ...... never driving processes by tweets and un-truths.

- Leaders need to be fully **supportive** of others and **dynami-cally connected**

  ...... never being overly driven by outside influences.

- Leaders need to be fully **committed** to their roles and po-tential outcomes

  ...... never being fraudulent or fake in that it fuels chaos.

➢ Leaders need to be **engaging**, **empathetic**, and **understanding** of challenges

...... never be uninvolved in shocking events and natural disasters.

➢ Leaders need to be **mature** and **professional**

...... never demonstrate immaturity and childlike behaviors.

➢ Leaders need to put all forms of **ego aside**

...... never look for personal compliments and selfish praise.

➢ Leaders need to constantly **learn** and **grow** to close emotional and mental gaps

...... never believe that all business knowledge is fully known.

➢ Leaders need to show **confidence** and **willingness** to handle challenges

...... never showing insecurity and strategic dysfunctionality.

➢ Leaders need to grow and build **trust** along with **optimism**

...... never be untruthful, unstable, or irrational with behaviors.

➢ Leaders need to be **consistent** and **engaged** in their personal leadership style

...... never be chaotic or foolish with actions and communication.

- ➢ Leaders need to have **global knowledge** and **insights**
  ...... never be ignorantly unconscious and decon-structing structure.

- ➢ Leaders need to be **humble** and **proud** of their leadership position
  ...... never be solely focused on oneself and disre-spectful of the role.

- ➢ Leaders need to be fully **self-aware** of their competencies and abilities
  ...... never be ignorant regarding the impact of be-haviors and approaches.

- ➢ Leaders need to drive **creativity** and **innovative activities**
  ...... never accepting the status-quo and non-mean-ingful work.

To be effective, a leader needs to be self-aware of their own personal capabilities and to have a clear sense of purpose. Their credibility and trust building are based on personal confidence and the ability to move beyond the unknown. Success comes from critical-thinking and risk-taking by the leader to address key challenges and global issues with a full handle on their emotional and psychological makeup.

Leaders need to be courageous and self-assured. They need to empower others and make the employee population feel fully engaged by encouraging involvement and recognizing commitment to the organization. They need to have appreciation and enthusiasm for valued and innovative results. And, effective and impactful leaders must inspire the pursuit of a common vision with energy and optimism for a real and meaningful future.

Without a doubt, it is imperative to accept the fact that leaders are operating in a time of turbulence. Leaders must use competency strengths and attitudes to energize others. They need to learn to align all leadership components to drive growth, profitability, engagement, commitment, and satisfaction. It is an opportunity to embrace change and fully engage in leadership transformations that encourage enthusiasm for a progressive future. Leaders need to balance open humility and assertive behaviors so that it can ignite innovative curiosity along with long-term commitments. Leaders need to learn to navigate tensions in business during times of uncertainty and transition. Clearly, actions need to result in outcomes that are beyond the status quo. Leaders must have courage to look at all business challenges with a willingness to be vulnerable as well as to take responsibility for risk. Basically, leaders need to manage and lead the present with a vision for shaping the future.

Remember, true leadership is based on *human chemistry* and is about self-leadership ... expecting the most of oneself. This is based on self-awareness. Always model the values and attitudes that one would expect from others. Have humility, be accountable, and be responsible for oneself as a skillful, passionate, and purposeful leader.

- Elevate engagement
- Actively listen from the heart
- Help others accomplish goals
- Build on past experiences
- Delegate decision-making power
- Praise achievements

The Chemistry of LEADERSHIP

Throughout your leadership learning journey and by reading this book, I hope you have been able to make many self-discoveries and have found the leader in you.

General Wisdom

The Preface to Frederic Hudson's/Pamela McLean's book — *Life Launch – A Passionate Guide to the Rest of Your Life* – closes with a personal reflection by Frederic on his "Wake-up call – lessons learned" "awakening" at the age of 9 in 1943. His nurse, Susan, provided a <u>Simple description on wisdom</u> specific to dealing with his paralyzing polio (which he recovered from after several months in the hospital). (26)

- *See how you want your life to unfold.*
- *Look for your best choices.*
- *Trust your vision.*
- *Create a detailed plan to get you from here to there.*
- *Take full responsibility for your life course: time manage every detail.*
- *Find the best resources available for empowering your future. Network, train, travel, and seek adventure.*
- *Learn how to learn, unlearn, and relearn. Make learning your central business.*
- *Live on the outer edge of your possible reaches, not on the inner edge of your security.*

My Personal Wisdom

- ❖ Always find the good and positive in everything.
- ❖ Use past learnings to build future experiences.
- ❖ Make careful choices and turn dreams into reality.
- ❖ Accept challenges and stretch the innovative imagination.
- ❖ Learn and grow from the contributions of others.
- ❖ Appreciate the love and support of a spouse and children.

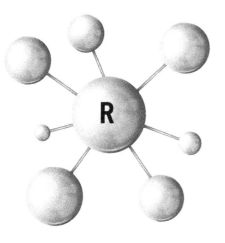

REFERENCES
AND BIBLIOGRAPHY

Chapter One

(1) Book: *Firms of Endearment – How World-Class Companies Profit from Passion and Purpose*

- Rajendra Sisodia, Jagdish N. Sheth, David Wolfe

- New rules that transform business from the inside out

- Second Edition / 2014 / Pearson Education Press, New Jersey

Chapter Two

(1) Article: *Building Your Company's Vision*

- James C. Collins and Jerry I. Porras

- Harvard Business Review / September-October 1996 / #96501-PDF-ENG

(2) Video: *Empathy: The Human Connection to Patient Care*

- YouTube / Cleveland Clinic / 4:24 / February 2013

(3) Book: *The Speed of Trust: The One Thing that Changes Everything*

- Stephen M.R. Covey

- Franklin Covey Press

(4) Book: *The Trusted Edge – How Top Leaders Gan Faster Results, Deeper Relationships, and a Stronger Bottom Line*

- David Horsager

- Free Press – Division of Simon & Schuster, NY, NY / 2012

(5) Book: *True North: Discover Your Authentic Leadership*

- Bill George and Peter Sims

- Jossey-Bass / 2007 / ISBN 978-0787987510

Chapter Three

(1) Paper: *Critical Thinking in General Chemistry*

- Leonard S. Kogut – Professor of Chemistry - Penn State Beaver Campus, Monaca, PA

- Journal of Chemical Education – March 1996 / Volume 73 – Number 3

(2) Quote by Henry Ford

- Founder of the Ford Motor Company / Henry Ford – died April 7, 1947

(3) Quote by Grace Speare

- Author of *Everything Talks to Me: The True Story of a Successful Search for Enlightment*

Chapter Four

(1) Quote from Antointe de Saint-Exupery

- Author of *The Little Prince* / de Saint-Exupery died July 31, 1944

(2) Model: Wilson Learning Social Style Matrix

- A model focused on managing interpersonal relationships
- Wilson Learning – Minneapolis, MN

Chapter Five

(1) Video: *Good Chemistry – Bonding* / On YouTube

- Montessori Muddle / Posting by Lensyl Urbuno

(2) Quote by Oscar Wilde

- Irish poet and playwright in the 1880s and 1890s / London, UK

(3) Book: *Reclaiming Conversations – The Power of Talk in a Digital Age*

- Sherry Turkle
- Penguin Books / October 2015 / ISBN13: 9780143100792

(4) Model: The GRPI Model

- 1977 – Rubin, Plovnick, Fry / Model for team cooperation and development

- First introduced 1972 – Richard Becklard

(5) Quote from Gallup Organization

- American research-based, global performance-management consulting company

- Washington, DC / Founded 1935

(6) Book: *Grateful Leadership – Using the Power of Acknowledgement to Engage All Your People and Achieve Superior Results*

- Judith W. Umlas

- McGraw-Hill Education / November 2012

(7) Model: A bicycle analogy model

- Detailed in Lance H.K. Secretan's book: *Reclaiming Higher Ground*

- Macmillan Canada / 1997

(8) Model: SMART

- *Management Review* – November 1981 – by George Doran

- Goal components and represented acronym – S.M.A.R.T.

(9) Book: *What Got You Here Won't Get You There – How successful people became even more successful*

- Marshall Goldsmith

- Published by Hyperion – 2007

(10) Quote from Marshall Goldsmith

- From his book *What Got You Here Won't Get You There*

(11) Article: *Violinist Joshua Bell played incognito in a Washington subway*

- Washington Post – April 2007

(12) Book: *Overcoming the Five Dysfunctions of a Team: A Field Guide for Leaders, Managers, and Facilitators*

- Patrick Lencioni
- Published by Wiley / 3/11/2005 / ISBN-10 0787976377

(13) Product – BETABRACE Reinforcing Composite / "Adding strength without adding weight"

- Dow Automotive / Auburn Hills, MI

(14) Story – from Character Quality Stories

- *Woman at Airport Waiting Area at another's Man's Cookies by Mistake*

Chapter Six

(1) Book: *The Art of the Long View – Planning for the Future in an Uncertain World*

- Peter Schwartz / A Currency Paperback – Published by Doubleday / 1991 / 1996

(2) Quote by the Dalai Lama

- Monk of the Gelug School / Tibetan Buddhism

(3) Quote by Albert Einstein

- German-born theoretical physicist / Lived from 1879 to 1955

(4) Book: *Grateful Leadership - Using the Power of Acknowledgement to Engage All Your People and Achieve Superior Results*

- Judith W. Umlas

- McGraw-Hill Education / November 2012

(5) Quote by Sardek Love

- President & Founder of Infinity Consulting and Training Solutions

- Manassas, VA

(6) Book: *Synchronicity: The Inner Path of Leadership*

- Joseph Jaworski / 1996

(7) Newsletter – *The Leadership Challenge* / John Wiley & Sons Inc

- April 2017 / James Kouzes and Barry Posner

(8) Model: Wilson Learning Social Style Matrix

- A model focused on managing interpersonal relationships

- Wilson Learning – Minneapolis, MN

(9) Book: *Leader is an Art* by Max de Pree

- A Currency Book / Published by Doubleday / 1989 / ISBN: 0-385-512-46-5

(10) Model – Johari Window – A Psychological Tool

- Created in 1955 by Joseph Luft (1916 – 2014) and Harrington Ingham (1916 – 1995)

- Focused on helping people understand relationships with themselves

Chapter Seven

(1) Quote by Frederic Hudson, Ph.D. – Author of *The Handbook of Coaching – A Comprehensive Resource Guide for Managers, Executives, Consultants, and Human Resource Professionals*

- Published by Jossey-Bass / 1999

(2) Model – G-R-O-W – Developed in the UK / Used in coaching 1980's and 1990's

- First published in *Coaching for Performance*
- Graham Alexander / Sir John Whitmore

(3) Model – G-R-O-W – Developed in the UK / Used in coaching 1980's and 1990's

- First published in *Coaching for Performance*
- Graham Alexander / Sir John Whitmore

(4) Book: *Coaching for Leadership – How the World's Greatest Coaches Help Leaders Learn*

- Marshall Goldsmith / Laurence Lyons / Alyssa Fres

(5) Book: *Good to Great – Why Some Companies Make the Leap...and Other's Don't*

- James C. Collins
- Harper Business / October 2001 / ISBN-10 0066620992

(6) Book: *Good to Great – Why Some Companies Make the Leap...and Other's Don't*

- James C. Collins

- Harper Business / October 2001 / ISBN-10 0066620992

(7) Book: *Good to Great – Why Some Companies Make the Leap...and Other's Don't*

- James C. Collins

- Harper Business / October 2001 / ISBN-10 0066620992

(8) Article from *Coaching at Work*

- March / April Issue

(9) Survey: Chartered Institute of Personnel & Development - CIPD

- Professional association for human resource management

- Headquartered in Wimbledon, England / Founded in 1913

(10) Consulting organization – Right Management / ManpowerGroup

- Global career management and talent strategists

- Established in 1980 / Philadelphia, PA

(11) Consulting organization – Manchester Consulting Group

- Manchester, MA

(12) Report – *Coaching Executive Summary* / Right Management

- *What's the Quantifiable Return on Investment – 2004*

(13) The Center for Effective Organizations / Los Angeles, CA / Founded 1979

- Marshall School of Business / University of Southern California

- The CEO conducts cutting-edge research on a broad range of organizational effectiveness issues.

(14) Capital One Financial Service

- Founded 1988 / Richmond, VA

(15) Survey: *What Coaching Can and Cannot Do for Your Organization*

- Documented in the Journal of the Human Resource Planning Society

- Volume 30 / Issue 2 – 2007

(16) Article: *Planning as Learning* by Aria de Geus / Executive for Shell Oil Company

- Harvard Business Review – March/April 1988

- De Geus from Rotterdam, Netherlands – a Dutch business executive and business theorist.

- Managing uncertainty – Five pages / #88202-PDF-ENG

Chapter Eight

(1) Consultant – DDI – Development Dimensions International

- Published leadership competencies in Wall Street Journal – 2011

- An international human resource and leadership development consultancy

- Founded 1970 / Bridgeville, PA

(2) Book: *Leaders Don't Command – Inspire Growth, Ingenuity, and Collaboration*

- Jorge Cuervo / ATD Press / 2015 / ISBN – 10:1-56286-935-3

Chapter Nine

(1) Myers-Briggs Assessment Tool / Instrument

- MBTI Type Indicator – An introspective self-report questionnaire designed to indicate psychological preferences in how people perceive the world and make decisions.

- Foundation located in Gainesville, FL

(2) FIRO-B Assessment Tool / Instrument

- Fundamental Interpersonal Relations Orientation – Behavior

- Measures interpersonal needs on three scales: Inclusion, Control, and Affection

- Psychometrics Canada Ltd – Edmonton, AB

(3) Human Synergistics Assessment Tool / Instrument

- Field of organizational development for more than 45 years

- Focuses on pioneering culture insights / Tool – The Circumplex

- Plymouth, MI and Chicago, IL

(4) Blake & Mouton's Management Grid

- Based on two behavioral dimensions – Concern for People / Concern for Results

- Leadership Dilemmas, Houston, TX

(5) Hertzberg Assessment Tool / Instrument

- Built by Fredrick Hertzberg – psychologist

- Motivating teams and leadership assessments

(6) DDI Assessment Tool / Instrument

- Development Dimensions International – Founded in 1970 by William Byham

- Human resource and leadership development consultancy – Bridgeville, PA

(7) OPQ32 Assessment Tool / Instrument

- CEB (formally SHL) – Occupational Personality Questionnaire

- The most widely used measure of behavioral style in the world

(8) DiSC Assessment Tool / Instrument

- Behavioral assessment tool built by William Moulton, psychologist

- Traits – dominance, influence, steadiness, and compliance

(9) TDF Assessment Tool / Instrument

- Talent Assessment – to help team work more effectively together

(10) IOL Assessment Tool / Instrument

- Management consulting out of Stockholm, Sweden

(11) Frances Hesselbein Leadership Institute

- Publishes *Leader to Leader* via Jossey-Bass / New York, NY

(12) Quote: Marcel Proust – French novelist (1872 – 19922)

- Novelist, critic, and essayist

- One of the most influential authors of the 20th century

(13) Getinge Group Portfolio – A Talent Management Portfolio entitled *The Getinge Way*

- 100-page booklet with nine sections

(14) Getinge Group Portfolio

- A Talent Management Portfolio entitled *The Getinge Way*

- 100-page booklet with nine sections

(15) Quote: Steve Garvey

Former professional baseball player (Dodgers) and current Southern California businessman.

(16) Quote: Peter F. Drucker

- Austrian-born American management consultant, educator, and author

- Awarded Presidential Medal of Freedom – 2002

(17) Quote: by Mary Angelou

- American poet, memorist, and civil rights activist / lived from 1928 – 2014

(18) Quote from the Gallup Organization

- American research-based, global performance-consulting company

- Founded by George Gallup in 1935 / Washington, DC

(19) Quote – Aristotle

- Ancient Greek philosopher and scientist / Lived 384 BC – 322 BC

- Father of Western Philosophy

(20) Quote by Larry Bossidy

- Businessman and author / Retired CEO of AlliedSignal

(21) Book – *The Speed of Trust: The One Thing that Changes Everything - 2006*

- Stephen M.R. Covey

- Free Press / Division of Simon & Schuster / ISBN-13 978-0-7432-973-1

(22) Book – *Leadership is an Art* – Max de Pree

- A Currency Book / Published by Doubleday – 1989 / ISBN 0-385-512 46-5

(23) Book – *The Power of Thanks – How Social Recognition Empowers Employees and Creates a Best Place to Work*

- Eric Mosley and Derek Irvine

- McGraw Hill Education / 2014 / ISBN 978-0-07-183840-5

(24) Book - *Grateful Leadership – Using the Power of Acknowledgement to Engage All Your People and Achieve Superior Results*

- Judith W. Umlas

- McGraw-Hill Education / November 2012

(25) Book – *Presence – Bringing your Boldest Self to your Biggest Challenges* / 2015

- Amy Cuddy

- Little, Brown & Company / Hachette Book Co. / ISBN 978-0-316-25657-5

(26) Book – *Life Launch – A Passionate Guide to the Rest of Your Life*

- Frederic Hudson / Pamela McLean

- The Hudson Institute of Santa Barbara, CA

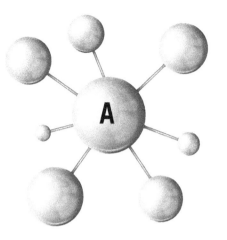

ABOUT THE AUTHOR
PAUL E. FEIN

Paul has had many outstanding career experiences and educational learning accomplishments as a part of his life-long leadership journey. He has been a dedicated and creative contributor in positions that he has held both in education and in business.

- A people educator and professional executive builder.
- A custom-crafter of growth-oriented leadership workshops.
- A dynamic speaker and engaging development program facilitator.
- A certified career-life coach and management mentor.
- A creative writer and inspiring educational innovator.

Paul has been fully committed to driving development and growth of others. He has built his personal competencies and capabilities based on a diverse career journey – teaching high school chemistry, marketing management within several manufacturing industries, and global executive leadership development facilitation. Throughout these work experiences, he continued to grow his skills through post-educational programs at University of Southern California, Harvard Law, Cornell University, and Copenhagen Business School. Coaching certification was achieved at the Hudson Institute in Santa Barbara, California.

Before establishing a consulting practice, he was responsible for human resource and learning development activities for a medical device company with its headquarters in Sweden. His primary responsibilities were focused on global talent management processes – ranging from performance management, succession planning, and high potential identification, to learning and development, and talent acquisition. He supported corporate initiatives specific to employee engagement, employer branding, and executive development.

Currently, Paul is the Managing Leader & Director of the IDD Leadership Group LLC – New York. He creates and facilitates leadership workshops and provides career-life coaching. His driving philosophy is to INSPIRE innovative imagination, DRIVE ideas into actions, and DELIVER strategic growth – always focused on enhancing individual and organizational effectiveness.

CPSIA information can be obtained
at www.ICGtesting.com
Printed in the USA
BVHW031154170220
572573BV00001B/16

9 781478 799245